GOD

and

The Twelve Problems of Evil

GOD

and

The Twelve Problems of Evil

———

Into Great Mystery

by

THOMAS RONALD VAUGHAN

RESOURCE *Publications* · Eugene, Oregon

GOD AND THE TWELVE PROBLEMS OF EVIL
Into Great Mystery

Resource Publications
An Imprint of Wipf and Stock Publishers
199 W. 8th Ave., Suite 3
Eugene, OR 97401

www.wipfandstock.com

PAPERBACK ISBN: 978-1-7252-6671-1
HARDCOVER ISBN: 978-1-7252-6672-8
EBOOK ISBN: 978-1-7252-6673-5

Manufactured in the U.S.A.   06/05/20

I form the light and create darkness, I make peace and create evil.

—ISAIAH 45:7 (KJV)

The creation was subjected to futility by God.

—ROMANS 8:20

The Lord said to Satan, "Have you considered my servant Job?"

—JOB 1:8

We enter the kingdom through many tribulations.

—ACTS 14:22

We see through a glass darkly.

—1 CORINTHIANS 13:12

Let my heart be broken with the things that break the heart of God.

—ROBERT PIERCE

And God shall wipe away every tear.

—REVELATION 21:4

quod iustus Deus—"God shall be vindicated."

—LATIN PHRASE

Contents

Camus and Eternal Sisyphus

One of the most disturbing endings to any book must be this last sentence written by one Albert Camus: We "must imagine Sisyphus happy."[1]

On January 4, 1960, near the small town of Villeblevin, France, Camus died in an automobile accident. He was only 46 years old. Two years earlier he had won the Nobel Prize in Literature, then the second youngest recipient in history. The world has wondered what he could have written had he lived.

"Literature" is actually an inexact designation for Camus' writings, which deal primarily with a philosophy of existence. As a self-declared atheist, he thought life was ultimately meaningless, but should nevertheless be lived with vigor, determination, and fearless resignation. He wrote a great deal about all of this in his novels.

The quote above is from his famous essay, "The Myth of Sisyphus." In it he retells the story of the tragic King Sisyphus of Greece, who was condemned to roll a huge rock to the top of a forbidding hill. But his labor was not complete, for inevitably the rock rolled back down. Poor Sisyphus had to repeat this excruciating task for all eternity. He was paying for his "sins." His condemnation was everlasting.

---

1. Quoted in ". . .One Must Imagine Sisyphus Happy," by Katerina Drina, Hektoen International Journal, Winter, 2018. The original edition of Camus' The Myth of Sisyphus was published in France, by Editions Gallimard in 1942.

The story was perfect for Camus since it demonstrates the utter futility of human life. And it was also important for his belief that in the face of this absurdity, humans could press on, and in so doing be "happy." Whether these arguments resonate convincingly with anyone is a secondary matter here, but in his literary output Camus describes a remarkable heroic atheism. Sisyphus was an incomparable figure to portray the existential reality of "a man against absurdity." Camus ends this essay with beautiful prose: "I leave Sisyphus at the foot of the mountain. One always finds one's burden again . . . The struggle itself . . . is enough to fill a man's heart. One must imagine Sisyphus happy."[2]

Certainly, one could review the French writer's life to decide if "heroic" is the correct summation, or if, indeed, his heart was "full." But no one should deny that Camus lived with passion, and often high purpose. The world he saw was filled with terror, dread, chaos, and ultimately, death. But he daily went about his affairs despite having concluded in advance that all was futile and absurd. There is nobility in that by any accounting.

As a Christian minister writing about God and the Problem of Evil, why would I begin with an essay on the famous atheist, Albert Camus? Surely it would be instructive to determine why he came to believe that there was no source from which life could obtain any meaning whatsoever. And I am writing about twelve manifestations of evil which can unarguably and decidedly snatch meaning from both life and faith.

I am, rather, interested in something else: Camus popularized an ancient myth and legend in which appears the ideal metaphor for the ceaseless, arduous intellectual and spiritual struggle with the Problem of Evil. It is a thing intractable. No one can resolve it. We expend our finest and our best, and if we move "the stone" at all, it comes crashing back down again. We start over!

This may sound overdone and needlessly dramatic. But anyone who begins this study will determine soon enough that they have undertaken a demanding, daunting task. There is help and comfort, however. We who begin are neither Greeks nor royalty.

2. Drina. ". . .One Must. . ." Quoting Camus

We are Christians. So regardless of outcome or result, we take our strength of will and energy to proceed directly from God. We will need both: this mountain and this rock are very real.

Einstein's Question

Albert Einstein once famously wrote, "What really interests me is whether God could have created the world any differently."[1] He was wondering about the laws of physics and the cosmic blueprint. He was not wondering about theology.

Physicists have a delightful way of asking whether the cosmos is the outcome of "law" or whether "law" is the outcome of the cosmos. Is there any such thing as "law," or is "law" simply a description of what actually "happens" repeatedly? The argument goes on. Either way, they really do not seem to enjoy pondering the origin of those natural laws, or why these laws and not others. That question is probably too philosophical or perhaps too theological. We were told in elementary school that that was precisely what science was supposed to do—look into the origin of things in order to better understand it all. Perhaps that has changed!

Of course, some believe in a multiverse, declaring that in another universe, laws may not be the same as they are in ours. That theory cannot be disproved, and is all very interesting. But for most Christian thinkers that interest is purely esoteric and in the end matters not at all. We live and die in this particular world, not another about which we can speculate.

Einstein did not believe in a Creator God, so his use of the word "God" has nothing much to do with Christian theology. Anyone can use that word, and many do so. But Einstein's question from

---

1. Quoted in "Did God Have a Choice?," by Dennis Overbye, New York Times, 1999

physics is surely this: was God under some "necessity" in creating the world? When we pause to consider the issues we are dealing with in this book, the question does come back with a resounding jolt. Could God have created this world in a different way? Why would we ask that? Because this world is filled with much that is wonderful and good, but it is also filled with an inordinate amount of evil. Could God have created another world without so much misery and woe? Or, is this the best of all possible worlds?

The Best Possible World?

There is a long and venerable history of wonderment and puzzlement at the frightening, even punishing nature and character of this, our inhabited world. That concern runs straight through the entire Bible. Adam's self-defense, the Book of Job, and the Psalms of Protest come instantly to mind. In Romans 8:22, the Apostle Paul says this creation is in bondage and is groaning. He means that the whole planet suffers deeply from various evil maladies.

In the New Testament, the heart-wrenching cry of Jesus from the cross, "My God, my God, why have you forsaken me?," is the capstone verse. Why, indeed, did the world created by Father God deal so treacherously and crushingly with his beloved children, the Only Begotten Son, and every living creature? Given this most honest Biblical assessment, we clearly have permission to ask the deep theological and philosophical questions about a holy, loving God creating the good earth intermixed with pervasive evil.

Gottfried Wilhelm Leibnitz was a great mathematician and passionate philosopher. In his writings he coined the term, "theodicy," which roughly means justifying God's eternal love with the ubiquitous evil in the world. Since this whole questioning enterprise originates in the mind of persons, theodicy may also be defined as "justifying the ways of God to mankind [sic]."

The idea is not that humans can cross-examine God, but that they nevertheless engage this troubling issue with their best intellectual skill and precise logical thought.

Leibnitz thought deeply about God, evil, and the world. He also penned an equally famous line, which is directly related to our study: "this is the best of all possible worlds." His thinking here was complicated and somewhat convoluted, but he concluded that evil was "necessary" because humans were finite, and needed to learn the good by contrast with this evil. Furthermore, and this is crucial, he said that since God could obviously conceive of, and choose from, all possible worlds, she chose this one. And, since God is infinitely good, this must be the absolute best choice: this is the best of all possible worlds.

Leibnitz seems to have concluded that the notion of the best of all possible worlds "solved" the problem of theodicy, the Problem of Evil. To him, it was the philosophical and theological solution sought after for ages.

I have no interest in delving into Leibnitzian thought, nor to point out where his logic breaks down disastrously. But I do have ongoing interest in the subject he was contemplating and the conclusions he reached. Is Leibnitz right? Is this the best of all possible worlds? I am quite sure that it is not, and I am certain that Leibnitz was wrong. But I pose this question: what if Leibnitz were right? If so, what is this the best possible world for?

Some theologians and philosophers have latched on to Leibnitz' claim and have directly or indirectly tried to defend it. Of course, they are concerned to defend God more than defend the 17th century genius. Their arguments echo his in declaring that the world provides the perfect environment in which to exercise free will, overcome evil, and grow into personal and spiritual maturity. This is a variation on the "instrumental view." Evil is an instrument used by God to accomplish spiritual ends.

No one doubts that evil must be viewed instrumentally. But limits must be set on that kind of analysis. Do we truly need "this much" evil through which to grow and mature? Is it not true that there is, beyond doubt, an overwhelming amount of evil—in all its manifestations? And this as well: is there much statistical evidence to indicate that large numbers of people, including Bible believers, are taking advantage of the contents of "the best of all possible worlds" in order to mature and flourish spiritually? I, of course, can answer my own questions, as can anyone giving this matter a moment's serious thought.

But I must add this, regrettably: millions of persons do not use the world for any purpose other than to, in short, create more evil. This planet is undeniably a grand place for "sinners" to sin, and that quite boldly.

Unfortunately, neither Leibnitz nor his followers help us here. And, quite frankly, anyone who believes in a better world to come, de facto believes that this is not the best possible world. Certainly, many thoughtful persons can contemplate additions and subtractions, and thereby create a better, more perfect world. Fantasy writers do it all the time. All daydreams can do that!

The Book Demands Reasons

I will begin this study exactly where it will end: no Christian believer and thinker can leave the topic of The Problem of Evil with a statement like this, "I now have philosophically and theologically satisfying answers to why our good God allows all kind of evil." That will be true despite two thousand years of Christian theology dealing with the issue from every standpoint imaginable.

That historical writing is often brilliant and provocative. It contains brash protest or heartfelt tears. It stretches the limits of thought with imposing logic and profound conclusions. But, alas, the stout walls of this impenetrable fortress are not breached or broken. Theology alone cannot do it.

Philosophy alone cannot do it. It cannot be done by even the highest functioning of human intellect coupled with the most devout spiritual insight.

Why, then, do I boldly undertake to produce yet another book on this gnawing subject? I have my reasons.

ONE: The Problem has been a focus of my thinking since undergraduate days as a student majoring in Bible. One of my early, rather naive term papers was on the subject. I was, back then, conversant with the major literature. The Problem is still in the forefront of my thinking.

TWO: Christianity is a religion based upon Revelation which is then encountered by Reason. I think the commandment to "love God with all your mind" (Luke 10:27; Matt 22:37), contains the two elements—the God who reveals and the human mind which responds. The Problem of Evil is not answered and explained in Revelation. Reason has not, nor can, resolve the matter. Yet, the Problem invites and demands inquiry by its very nature as a "given."

THREE: Christians, and all peoples, are affected by evil in all of its manifestations. It is, therefore, quite worthwhile—even if unwelcome—to keep the topic at the front of all Christian thinking. The history of the world, down to the headlines in today's news, display and catalog large and small occurrences of evil. Those are the things to which Christians must respond. Serious believers should always view this disturbing data as a theological issue, regardless of other ways of considering it. In these pages, I want readers to "think theologically" with me.

FOUR: I personally view the Problem as scientists view many realities that adversely affect our human well-being. For example, we all can list a dozen infirmities and diseases for which cures have not been found. The work heroically goes on. So, too, must "work" on this ever-present Problem. New insights, ideas, and definitions may aid us on our way.

FIVE: All literate Christians should be informed enough to articulate the basics of this crucially important faith Problem. I hope this book, written this particular way, can assist in that.

SIX: I understand that the Problem of Evil is often said to be the biggest obstacle to Christian belief. I dispute that because of my views on how one comes to faith in the first place. But I do not doubt its status in the larger arena of philosophy and theology. Non-believers may well point to this issue as a monumental hindrance to belief in the particular God we Christians proclaim. "How can you believe in a God who does nothing about evil in the world?" It is a commonplace question, and we must honestly admit that we cannot satisfactorily answer it for ourselves, much less for our critics. We must, therefore, find other ways to discuss the eternal significance of what we believe, even as we willingly locate this Problem squarely in that magnificent body of belief.

SEVEN: If Revelation does not answer, and if Reason cannot answer, what is left for believers? It is faith in a God of love.

Does faith empower us at all? And the answer is that faith is all that we have!

EIGHT: Faith is power enough for the Christian since this is the astonishing fact: our faith itself is a free, gracious gift from the very God of The Problem of Evil. We discover that despite the evil in our world—we still believe! We are totally convinced that our God is lovingly aware of our faith struggles with this Problem, and does more than we can ever imagine to sustain us in dealing with it.

NINE: Faith, however, as I define it, does not have an autonomous existence independent of Revelation and Reason. Some view faith as illogical, fanciful, mystical, and even anti-intellectual. But faith can be properly defined and given as much cognitive legitimacy as any other form of intellection. To show that is not my purpose here. Others have done it quite well. Blaise Pascal, no daydreaming intellectual lightweight, gave us the remarkable line: "The heart has its reasons" for its faith.

TEN: And because we believe deeply, we understand that this subject must be approached reverentially, even devotionally. The deep, dark issues are not to be skirted or minimalized, for they are part and parcel of all Christian Theology. We well know that The Problem of Evil is often given short shrift in our theology texts. That is not acceptable. It must be written about in bold relief and studied passionately. We join saints, living and dead, who wrestle with the demanding topic even prayerfully.

ELEVEN: I write this book as a "primer." There is, of course, the large, composite Problem which I attempt to separate and dissect into component parts. They can then be analyzed and understood in a useful, if overlapping sequence. The book title suggests this effort: The Twelve Problems of Evil.

TWELVE: In 1 John 5:4, the writer boldly declares that our faith is the victory that overcomes the world. The Problem of Evil is a mountainous, omnipresent part of the world. We cling to our "like precious faith" even as we understand well that "overcome" does not mean that we are given answers and solutions to all our profoundest concerns. That is nowhere promised in Holy Writ. We know some things about our God, but not everything. We know enough to walk by faith before both the mystery and the wonder. In so doing we may be able to transcend evil's effects and live as God's people. Christianity has always taught that believers cannot succumb to evil (Rom 12:21).

THIRTEEN: Perhaps I have said it above, but let me be crystal clear. I write to insist that Christians deal not only with human sin, but with every aspect of evil as it appears before us. Too long, Christians have focussed on individual sin and "personal salvation." We need not change that, but we must expand our horizons to see that unrestrained evil is all around, and that Christianity can be the powerful spiritual antidote. We do not have "all the answers," but we do have some! Faith can find creative, effective expression in multiple forms, and each one can confront and perhaps destroy evil. We are called to do just that.

FOURTEEN: This lengthy list is nearly complete. But I must register this as a highly significant reason why I wrote this book. I am convinced that the Problem of Evil is not a philosophical or theological abstraction originating from the thought and conclusions of such practitioners. I think, rather, that the Problem arises directly from Scripture itself, and presents itself from the earliest verses in Genesis all the way through the concluding chapters of the Revelation. Furthermore, the Problem must be laid squarely at the feet of our Lord God. I will visit these issues throughout the pages that follow, attempting to substantiate every claim about the text. The textual analysis inevitably leads to my theological and philosophical summations, but this is a "Biblical study" in every important respect.

The Vital Intersection

———

This reason for my writing demands a separate essay. I believe this book should speak to matters both personal and theological—for me and for all Christians who attempt to deal "pastorally" with the many issues related to these pervasive Problems. I mean, of course, lay persons and those ordained for ministry.

In my seminary years, and far beyond, I have heard many Christians say something that I can easily paraphrase: "I do not want to study theology. I just want to help people." Admittedly, there are theologies which ought not to be studied, unless one is interested in the larger topic called Historical Theology. But another point is being made by those professing such disdain for theology. They see a vast dichotomy between the rigors of that discipline and the practical aspects of a helping ministry.

I will not here attempt to persuade anyone to dig deeply into the meaty areas of theology—and there are some. I will simply affirm that all pastoral care must be built on a definable theological foundation. Without that, one may be practicing many socially useful things, but not Christian ministry.

I am not claiming that a book such as mine will provide that sufficient foundation. But I trust that readers will be challenged to clarify some of their critical thinking, so that their intentional ministries to persons will be better informed, more honest, and perhaps more effective. Confessionally, I have not been a faultless exemplar in modelling pastoral care. But I, like most believers, have too often confronted the Problems, and have been forced to "speak my faith" to them. I am therefore not alone; we Christians share this common bond.

Many pastors and laypersons can relate stories and events much like what I present here. As a second-year seminarian, I accepted a call to a student charge, two small churches in rural North Carolina. Shortly after beginning, I received a telephone message asking me to conduct my first funeral, for a 96-year old saint, suddenly deceased. That was relatively easy, and actually a time of worshipful celebration of, and gratitude for, a long life lived well. Though death in the abstract is an enemy (1 Cor 15:26), this home-going was not an issue for those of us dealing with the Problems of Evil. I would learn that not all funerals are so painless.

A few weeks later I officiated at the wedding of a lovely young woman and her Adonis husband. They were an amazing, handsome couple. Two weeks later, to the day, I buried the young man, killed instantly in a horrible trucking accident. My theological education and budding ministry were being baptized in the realities of life.

In Divinity School, I was becoming an ardent Universalist, and a Bible student quite comfortable with the interpretive methods of critical scholarship. I was acquiring some tools to use for intellectual pursuits, but also for life as a pastor. They would be needed, I discovered, for the rest of my earthly sojourn.

Life is a perplexing thing. I graduated from seminary and was ordained on May 31. On July 22, less than two months later, I buried our longed-for first child, a son, dead at the age of two and one- half hours. My wife and I were vacationing in her hometown when this occurred. In a few days we returned to the country parsonage shocked and damaged, only to learn that while we were away, a dear church couple had lost an eighteen-year old son in another frightening car crash. The thoughtful parishioners had not wanted to disturb us, those five hundred miles away. Another minister friend had kindly conducted the young man's sad service.

Why these stories? Every Christian can catalog similar events of heartache, tragedy, loss, and pain. Well do I know that. I have discussed only death and dying. I could easily write of inoperable cancer, dementia, birth defects, suicide, and all the other ingredients which are the daily fare of church members and their pastors.

I am making this point: these kinds of experiences are the highly visible intersection of theology and all helping ministry. At such scenes and places we must render the appropriate, compassionate care, but also think critically, deliberately, and Biblically. At this unwelcome and dreaded convergence, the Problems of Evil are revealed again and again, and become the raw data to be confronted by every Christian, layperson or ordained.

The Theology of the Problem of Evil is, therefore, not an abstract, ethereal intellectual pursuit in opposition to intentional, loving ministry. It is, rather, rooted, grounded, and ultimately defined by the everyday occurrences—the "stuff of life" for all people. Every Christian viscerally knows that someone, near or far, is always dealing with some aspect of the Problem of Evil. Without a Biblically- based theology through which to address this Problem, we are at the mercy of simplistic explanations which are not worthy of our Christian heritage.

God, Evil, And Christian Ambivalence

As important as any reason for my writing is this: The Problems of Evil present Christian believers with monumental cognitive challenges, but more than that, they can produce a very disquieting "faith-anxiety" that I call ambivalence. I will briefly explore that here.

There are any number of Biblical stories, scenes, and texts where this ambivalence appears glaringly. They well define what I am now discussing. The Book of Job is as good as any for illuminating the concern of this essay.

In Job 1:21, the battered and assaulted character declares, "Naked I came from mother's womb, and naked I shall return." There is nothing unusual about such an utterance, which could be made by anyone. But then he follows, "The Lord gave and the Lord took away." And Job 1:1–20 catalogs exactly what the poor man has had taken away by the "Lord": his health, his possessions, his children. This was an action of a supernatural being given permission by God to "test" the wretched Job. Job seems to understand this well enough, for his expression acknowledges the certain involvement of God. But it has a remarkable concluding phrase: "Blessed be the name of the Lord." (1:21)

Job's theology is fleshed out over the length of the long book. God becomes an Almighty mystery, an enemy, a friend, the deity of blessing and scourge. Job shouts such things as, "He destroys the blameless and the wicked" (9:22); "Let me alone, God" (10:20); "What do we gain by praying to God?" (21:15). James 5:11

comments on Job's "patience." We might use another term for this man's struggle to merely survive. Finally, he "comes to his senses," and finds God's renewed generosity compelling. He has passed the arduous "test"; all things are restored to him. The story ends. We have some answers, and many questions.

If anything is gleaned from this Book it is that human beings may well have life experiences that challenge and call into serious question any semblance of a rock solid, unshakeable faith in God. Job's reaction to this deity is confusion, rage, disdain, and worship. In this he models for many believers the most dreaded state of spiritual ambivalence: we fear God who metes out evil, we rage against God and the evil manifestations, but we know that we must and will conclude, "Blessed be the name of the Lord," as we worship obediently.

Christians have been woefully reluctant and painfully remiss in not recognizing and acknowledging this spiritual reality as a profound ingredient in the life of faith. It may be difficult for believers to admit that these "thoughts and feelings" are our own. It may be that they are displaced, suppressed, hidden away in a very understandable denial, which to confront would signal a frightening exposure of deeper things better left alone. Such a self-examination may leave us with unacceptable doubts about the genuine quality and quantity of faith itself.

In recent years a very popular song has appeared using Job 1:21 as an inspiration. Matt Redman's "Blessed Be Your Name" has the refrain, "You give and take away," but "blessed be your name." The lyrics remind that in time of trouble or triumph Christians are to bless God's name. I suspect, however, that like most songs and hymns utilized by worshippers over the years, this one is sung absent-mindedly, completely glossing over what is being said. What, indeed, had the Lord "taken away" in the story from which this jaunty tune derives: seven sons, three daughters, 7,000 sheep, 3,000 camels, 500 yoke of oxen, 500 donkeys, and a "large number of servants." In various and sudden ways, they were all killed instantly. "Blessed be the name of the Lord."

It is nearly impossible to characterize the spiritual and psychological makeup of a human being who could articulate such a response after enduring these unspeakable events. Job's spiritual immortality turns on this unlikely utterance. In later essays I will return with additional thoughts about this timeless narrative and its main character.

Dear Job, like many Christians after him, was visited in his time of trial by friends. They tried to tell him "what to do and what to think." It is a common human experience. They helped in some ways, not in others. At least they were physically present in an invaluable show of support. They were struggling, too.

Job's wife had had enough of the painful intensity of this divine visitation, and in her uncontrollable ambivalence verbalized the unthinkable: "Why don't you curse God and die!" (2:9). Job did not do that, though he said many things indicating his mental and spiritual anguish, things he might well regret on later reflection. In any event, we cannot judge too harshly any of the characters in this remarkable story. They were all mere mortals, overwhelmed by mysterious divine actions. They had few modern resources for "making sense" of any of these shocking events. The very fact that ancient writers created this Book tells all latter-day believers that the Problem of Evil is ageless, unsolvable, and may well forcefully insert itself into any life at any time. If there are ways to prepare for such occurrences, we do well to investigate what they are, always keeping on our lips, "Blessed be the name of the Lord."

Here, I am attempting to fill in a few blank pages in Christian theology. Certainly our personal response to God and evil is anything but constant faithfulness and untarnished trust. I am inviting others to contribute to our understanding of, and dealing with, this stark spiritual and psychological reality: ambivalence.

The Problems in Simple Terms

Christians have always believed many things about God, but certainly these two: our loving God is both transcendent and immanent. Something like this: God "oversees" the world and at the same time is also "active" in it. We are comfortable with the "oversees" part, as if a gracious Parent is above and outside, watching it all play out. But not to be accused of Christian Deism, we insist that she is also "active" here below.

And that is where the Problems of Evil begin. "If . . . why?," we ask. If God is truly immanent, and not just watching, why does our all-powerful, all-loving God not intervene more effectively in the troubling situations where humans are affected most? After all, God is agape love, and in basic, fundamental human understanding, love is supposed to act, not just observe.

We must go on. Every thoughtful Christian has also asked in doleful lament, "How does agape, the highest form of love, refuse to manifest itself when the very saints of God, following the dictates of their faith, are pleading and praying for legitimate succor and relief?" And because this does not occur, these struggling believers humbly demand to know how God can reassure that love is genuine now, and will be eternally.

There is another potent ingredient here. Since God obviously does not often involve himself observably and demonstrably "here below," how does God explain her palpable inaction? How are Christians to incorporate this deafening silence into a basic faith—theological understanding? What, truly, does the Bible say?

This is a forbidding number of questions thrown out in rapid-fire, and I apologetically reiterate that I would not be asking them had Scripture and Christian thinkers, over the past two thousand years, given adequate, satisfying answers. They have not! But they cannot be faulted for that, since there are no answers, only elucidations.

Average, faithful Christians need not ask questions the way I have here, but each believer is intuitively aware of the profound nature of their own Problems. Fortunately for all Christian witness, these dedicated followers understand full well that these Problems do not have to be "solved" before they attend to their daily ministrations in the hurting world. Responding to human need is relatively simple, even if the questions about the reasons for that need are not!

A Most Disturbing Question

A ll of my life I have heard it said that there are questions which ought not be asked. I understand the gist of the comment, generally speaking. However, in the realm of theology and philosophy I can think of no questions which categorically should not be asked.

There are great mysteries which lead to great questions: what is truth, beauty, justice, certainty? How can we even know another person? Why is there something instead of nothing? How will the world end? The list is a long one, and as curious thinkers we gravitate toward one topic over another, depending upon our interest or its perceived urgency in our lives.

As a Christian I am certain that there is no question that cannot be boldly and freely asked if indeed one is seeking legitimate spiritual truth and clarity. I repeat the venerable words about "faith seeking understanding." They present the time-honored and appropriate stance to take. However, and this is vital, Christians do not intend for understanding to replace faith. All new understanding becomes an integral part of the total reservoir of faith.

In asking questions and seeking answers we must remember a few more things. We are told that the word "mystery" appears twenty-eight times in the New Testament. Its essential meaning is that something hidden has now been revealed, at least in part. That is important, for it is not the case that where the word is employed everything being discussed is now so transparent that we have no additional questions or wonderments.

We are likely far less faithful and spiritual than the writers of Scripture. They said such things as these: there is the mystery of our faith (1 Tim 3:9); we can go deeper into the things of Christ (Heb 6:1); we see through a glass darkly (1 Cor 13:12). We tread slowly here as we realize with them that some things have been revealed, but much has not.

What more of our mysterious faith can we unveil and know? How much more should we know? We ask our questions carefully. But with the Problem of Evil, we confront one of the most disturbing questions which can be asked.

I suspect that most of us were first exposed to the "hard sciences" rather early in our education. We were told that one of the salutary roles of science was to discover how the universe "works." The more we learned about science, however, the more we realized that science is loathe to inquire into the "meaning" or "purpose" of this vast cosmos. Very brilliant scientists in all fields openly and vocally declare that the universe has no discernible purpose whatsoever. They use words like "meaningless" or "purposeless," but will often revert to the more disparaging terms "valueless" or "absurd." The irony of geniuses spending their lives on what they themselves profess to be ultimately absurd is not lost on anyone!

It follows suit that scientists have little interest in "origins." They openly acknowledge that they deal with everything at one remove. Behind the "everything" is, of course, origins: the laws of nature, the origin of life, the rise of consciousness, even the existence of the cosmos itself. But to spend time speculating on such topics seems to most scientists a waste of valuable inquiry and energy. The great biologist Charles Darwin stated it classically: "It is mere rubbish thinking of the origin of life."[1] Other scientists have voiced similar sentiments, often concluding that the search for these ultimate origins is just too philosophical or even downright theological.

---

1. Charles Darwin, "Letter to Joseph Dalton Hooker," March 29, 1863, quoted in "Charles Darwin and the Origin of Life," by Juli Pereto, Joseph L. Buda, Antonio Lazcano, *Origins of Life and the Evolution of the Biosphere*, Springer Publications, 2009

For Christians, that is exactly the point. The true believers then rush in with all kinds of theological ideas about those beginnings. They, of course, attribute almost all things to the Creator God. According to their faith, they are surely right to do so, even if many scientists—not all—openly scoff at the notion of a deity who puts all things in motion and sustains them through prevenient grace.

I said many Christians attribute "almost all" things to God. If scientists have their reasons for avoiding talk of origins, it unfortunately appears that many Christians do so as well. The one issue that greatly troubles their finest thinkers is this: what is the origin of evil?

Christians rightly urge scientists to be more honest, open, and thorough in speculating about origins in their respective fields of learning. But in the "theological sciences," believers seem to experience a genuine fear and reluctance to forge ahead on this roadblock subject. The reason for this is not far to seek: Can we possibly say that God created and sustains what we define as evil? After all, God created all things, as we are told repeatedly in Scripture. Can evil be one of those entities? Dare we ask?

Some may think the question is irreverent, taboo, or even sinful. But that is quite beside the point, since no question in all Christian theology obtrudes more into every area of life, for believers and non-believers. In coming essays I will boldly speculate about many aspects of this entire issue. I believe we can think theologically and Biblically through it all. What is the origin of evil? Let us see what is presented transparently in Scripture.

The Propositions

Each of the essays in this book will be more intelligible if "The Propositions" are read carefully, perhaps often. They are the focal point and locus for everything here. Thus, I can reassure my readers that though I may appear to follow some curious and circuitous routes, and to visit some very strange places, all the content eventually return to these premises as home base.

The Problems of Evil cast a large net which I believe covers all theological and philosophical inquiry. I intend for The Propositions to be that inclusive and expansive.

1. God is holy, agape love.

2. God in love creates and sustains all that exists.

3. God creates and sustains both good and evil.

4. Sin and evil are separable entities.

5. In the course of human maturation, all humans sin against God.

6. God cannot sin, even in creating and sustaining evil.

7. God demands that her children become holy (Lev 11:44, 1 Pet 1:15–16, et al.), and perfect (Matt 5:48).

8. Christian theology can incorporate the existence of evil which is commensurate with God's demands for holy perfection.

9. Christian theology cannot incorporate the existence of inordinate, overwhelming evil which is incommensurate with God's demands for holy perfection.

10. Hence, The Problem of Evil exists for that theology.

11. God's mysterious creation of evil inevitably and inextricably involves Godself in concomitant suffering.

12. God will, in eternity, destroy all evil, including sin, and eventually bring everyone into everlasting blessedness.

13. God determines that the eternal outcomes are "worth" the manifestations of evil in the lives of persons, animals, the world, and God's own Self.

Both Biblical theology and philosophy understand that "evil" is an abstract concept, not a "concrete reality." It is known and identified through its manifestations in the world. In this way it is similar to other abstractions, both positive and negative. These include mercy, justice, righteousness, love, hate, prejudice, discrimination, et al. My repeated use of the words "creates and sustains" is to be understood in this light. It is a usage common in Scripture where abstractions are mentioned.

Christians always prefer the notion that God "permits" or "allows" evil. That both God and evil exist in the world is irrefutable proof that the statement is true. Cognitive concerns arise when the term "inflicts" is attached to God and evil. This usage introduces the whole topic of human knowledge and the identification of "evidence" for any action of God. Though I make a few comments about this kind of topic throughout the book, the larger issues of truth claims, verifiability, and certainty are not my immediate interest here.

Naming The "Enemies"

There are several "End of the World" scenes in Scripture, and they cannot be harmonized. Paul attempts his own version in 1 Corinthians 15. It is an interesting procession of events, going from Christ raising the dead who belong to him, to Christ giving the Kingdom to "God the Father." This interim period, of unknown duration, allows Christ to destroy "all dominion, authority, and power," and then the last enemy, "death."

Paul is freely speculating here, and despite his visions and personal revelations, can have no certainty about the divine chronology for these spectacular events. His ideas do not match other expositions of the End, as found in the Gospel of Matthew, the Book of Revelation, or the Epistles of Peter.

Yet, his descriptions make perfectly good theological sense and offer suggestive ideas to those of us who are trying to unravel some of the deep mysteries involved in the larger Problem of Evil. Paul makes two important points. He clearly sees the destruction of all things, that are contrary to the will of God, in eschatological terms. It happens at the "End." And, secondly, he describes the things to be overcome as "enemies," impersonal enemies, not human creatures. His view resonates exactly with the vexing conclusion of those who study theodicy: the Problem will not be resolved by thought or action in our Common Era. It will be clarified only by God and only on God's timetable. Still, we can think along with Paul in attempting to identify and define these adversaries of God and her Kingdom.

In another book, the Apostle reassures the Colossians that Christ will be "disarming and overtaking" all powers, authorities, and principalities. According to 1 Corinthians, Christ's work will seemingly terminate with the demise of death, the "final" enemy.

Another scene can be added to that End. According to Psalm 110:1, God will crush all enemies under the feet of the Messiah. That verse is underscored in the New Testament, and must surely have been on Paul's mind when he penned 1 Corinthians 15:27. The Psalmist had written, "The Lord says to my Lord: 'Sit at my right hand until I make your enemies a footstool for your feet.'" Matthew 22:44 quotes the verse in its entirety. It asserts plainly that the humiliated and devastated enemies not only bow at the "Lord's" feet; they become a literal resting place for them!

If there are Twelve Problems of Evil, they will unquestionably join the dominions, authorities, powers, thrones, and all such enemies now crushed and prostrate at the holy feet of Christ. To "name" those Twelve Problems, we now turn.

The Twelve Problems Of Evil

What I now list under each Problem may be patently self evident, and is hardly an exhaustive cataloging of what could be there. I simply intend to demonstrate the multiplicity and complexity of issues that can be considered in defining each individual Problem. Perhaps there is a usefulness in viewing them separately, for when they rejoin in the composite Problem of Evil, their sheer magnitude can appear crushingly unmanageable, even inexorable.

Following this listing I continue with essays on interrelated topics, some specifically dealing with individual Problems. They, too, are not presented as complete or thorough explorations of the topics. They are purposely suggestive of where more indepth discussions might go.

Since I am defining these components as parts associated with the larger Problem, I note that they obviously overlap in sharing a common denominator: each can produce various kinds of harm, injury, hurt, suffering, death—evil to humans, other creatures, the planet, or to God herself. This overlap may be large or small.

The Twelve Problems of Evil

1. Human Sin: intentional, volitional violation, by thought, word, or deed, of known commandments of God. Such commands must be capable of being "kept" by human beings.

   The commands must be agreed as from God and not human creations. Discerning this will include agreement by the Community of Faith that they are teachings of Scripture, and are indeed divinely given. Acceptance of such teaching is ultimately a matter of individual conscience, as it is informed by that Scripture, the Holy Spirit, and the Faith Community.

To declare one a "sinner" is to affirm that the person is capable of intentional, volitional violation of God's commands. Non-believers are guilty of sin by the same definition, even if unaware of their standing before God. All humans are amenable to the commands of God.

A related aspect of this Problem is the human "sin nature," the notion that persons possess a propensity or strong tendency to sin. This concept relates to Christian Anthropology, and is pertinent only when sin is actually committed.

2. Human and Animal Suffering: physical and emotional pain experienced by either humans or animals. Humans can suffer spiritual pain in addition. Suffering is a term for pain more intense than the multiple forms of trivial pain, and can be caused by many different sources. Most of these can be identified in the Twelve Problems. Humans can experience suffering from situations and events which are of value to themselves, even if a matter of indifference to others.

3. Human and Animal Death: the ultimate termination of life, which may be brought about in many ways. In some instances death may be perceived as welcome due to the circumstances of the person or animal facing it. Humans may embrace death in a definition of "laying down one's life for friends." That life may end in either of these ways does not thereby reclassify the extinction of life as a "good" thing.

At some point in their development, human beings likely grasp the fact of their own mortality. Apparently young children and animals do not.

4. Transpersonal Sin: evil which can be perpetrated upon humans, animals, and the earth by impersonal means, attributable to no single person or groups of persons. While individual or corporate sin may initially create this evil, it can evolve into substantial suprapersonal and impersonal entities and realities. The numerous examples of this include unjust,

oppressive government and law, prejudice, racism, bigotry, acritical nationalism, nihilism.

Many of these transpersonal characteristics are included in such Biblical terms as "principalities, thrones, and powers." The ineffective workings of such institutions can produce the sin and evil of war, famine, genocide, inadequate healthcare, and oppression, including many actions which injure the planet and its animal inhabitants.

Most disease and plague originate transpersonally, as do other maladies such as birth defects, mental illness, neurological and physical impairment, and other chronic or debilitating conditions of both humans and animals.

5. Human Incompletion and Loss: unfulfilled human potential and loss of vitality due to a multiplicity of factors. The nearly limitless abilities of persons may be shriveled, wasted, or destroyed by mental and physical conditions, injury, addiction, illegal acts, abuse, lack of education or opportunity, and premature death. Humans may lose the means of production, income, education, mobility, property, place, reputation, et al.

    Incompletion and loss may occur with or without the experience of pain or suffering. Lost potential may involve large groups of persons, and affect nations, ethnicities, and races. Humans can imaginatively attribute this evil to animal species.

6. Human Affective Response: emotional and spiritual responses to all things affected by the Problems of Evil. Appropriate, positive responses include empathy, compassion, caring concern. Negative and unwelcome responses are frustration, rage, sadness, terror, fear, et al.

    Evil in the lives of humans, animals, and the planet may create a lifeless lethargy and a genuine paralysis expressed in "not knowing what to do." This reaction can culminate in obsessive, troubling memories, and can produce a pronounced ambivalence in one's faith positions. Certainly the capacity to experience and to express love may be affected by the evil surrounding human life. Guilt and shame are concomitant parts of the perception of inadequacy and ineffectiveness.

7. Human Cognitive and Intellectual Inadequacy: related to Problem 6, human limitations in intellectual ability to solve, resolve, and ameliorate the effects of evil in the lives of humans, animals and the planet. The composite Problem of Evil yields unsolvable problems and challenges to faith and belief. This reality may produce high levels of ambiguity and uncertainty, and a disquieting sense of the realistic limits of thought and cognition.

    Beyond faith matters, this inadequacy presents itself in the human inability to find "answers," resolutions, or cures for disease, war, poverty, famine, corruption, and issues related to sustaining the planet.

    As a result of this particular inadequacy, humans miscalculate, falsely accuse and attribute, make disastrous decisions, fail in planning analysis, solving crime, etc., often with catastrophic results. Where this occurs in geopolitics, costly wars can result, with tragic consequences for decades.

8. False Views of Good and Evil: the human tendency, intentionally or unintentionally, to redefine evil, to deny its existence altogether, or to call evil good. There is no unanimous agreement among Christians as to the singular definition of either good or evil. Nor is there among non-believers.

    Evil is a term which presupposes a judgment made from a position transcending the immediate reality. It is, therefore, a valuational determination. Christians assume that God is the ultimate and eternal "valuing entity," who is both immanent in and transcendent above all activity on the created earth. God has revealed himself in history, and revelations of his "valuations" are contained in Holy Writ. All views of and opinions about evil must find their definitions in those pages.

    Humans who do not believe in a God, or in the God of revelation, may find evil a useless or unnecessary term, thus denying the entire legitimacy of addressing the Problem of Evil.

It is clearly the case that good can be called evil or evil good. Much evil has been created by persons, governments, and institutions incorrectly defining their actions as good, even claiming that they are the will and word of God.

9. Natural Evil: natural occurrences causing harm, suffering, or death to living beings. These happenings have been called "Acts of God," and include earthquake, lightening, storm, fire, flood, tsunami, etc. They are normal events for nature, and may also cause no appreciable harm.

    Instinctual behavior among animals cannot be termed evil, though it obviously can contribute to their suffering and death. Some such animal behaviors may inadvertently cause their injury or death. In nature, microbes, insects, mammals, non-mammals, etc., may likewise cause harm, injury, or death among themselves, or to humans.

10. Degradation of the Planet: any harm to flora, fauna, earth, sea, or sky caused by any of several reasons. Examples include deforestation, pollution, over-fishing or hunting, habitat and breeding ground destruction, sprawling cities, or any occurance which damages the ecosystem. This degradation may result from human sin, natural events, or transpersonal sin.

11. Temptation to Sin and to Create Evil: in humans, the inner prompting to sin or to perpetrate harm, suffering, or death upon humans, animals, or the planet. Temptation per se is not sin or evil; acting upon it is contrary to the commandments of God.

    Temptation can arise from deprivation or from plenty, and is a common phenomenon among believers and non-believers. Theologically, "moderate" temptation seems to be a necessary ingredient for spiritual maturation, with growth occurring through the act of resisting the temptation. Tempting factors vary greatly among humans.

12. God's Suffering Involvement in Evil: the suffering of God Almighty caused by her intentional immanental, passionate, and compassionate involvement in the lives of humans, animals, and the planet. Humans understand God's suffering analogically, and discover its reality in the anthropomorphic language of Scripture. This suffering is defined by, and ultimately subsumed in, God's eternal agape love. Any theological position declaring that God does not or cannot suffer is heresy and in itself evil.

What About The Devil?

I have just stated that God both creates and sustains evil. Many might respond that such a blanket assertion fails to account for the existence of the Devil, or Satan. I am well aware of that, and I will express my views on the matter now. These comments will help clarify other things I say throughout the book.

My fundamental point is this: I see no Biblical, theological, philosophical, or metaphysical reason to posit the existence of a wholly evil being who has ontological status as do humans. I see no logical difference between declaring that God both creates and sustains evil, and declaring that God both creates and sustains the existence of the Devil who perpetrates this evil.

I can make several related points.

1. Affirming the existence of the Devil changes nothing in defining the essence of the Problem of Evil: God is ultimately responsible for evil.

2. If God does not create and sustain evil, then, by definition a.) a being must exist who creates evil ex nihilo, or, b.) God empowers such a being so to do.

3. The notion of any evil entity who was not created by God, but exists from eternity with God, is a heresy, abhorrent to Christian faith.

4. Introducing the existence of a wholly evil, nearly omnipotent Devil turns Christianity into a mythological religion similar to those of ancient Greece, Rome, the Middle East,

or the Norse. God battles with an Evil One, and for some unexplained reason, the struggle involves the entirety of an unwitting human race. The eternal goals of the conflict are vague, but appear to be related to rule and sovereignty over the cosmos, earth, and the salvation or damnation of human creatures. God seems not to be willing or able to convince the Devil to "cease and desist," even after God declares the ultimate defeat and utter destruction of all evil. Oddly, the all-powerful God is content to define the history of the cosmos in terms of this battle, which God could end at any moment. How God and the Devil are actually engaging each other is impossible to identify from any human perspective.

5. Affirming the existence of the Devil is minimally an effort to distance God from the manifestations of evil in the world, thus ensuring that the Devil is the intermediary conduit for perpetrating that evil.

6. It is plausible that the ancient Hebrew scribes did not believe in a literal Devil, but brilliantly created a composite being to give a reasonable, rational explanation for the existence of sin, evil, and the calamity in the world.

7. Further evidence of this is that in almost all of their subsequent history, no mention is made of the Devil's influence, presence, or activity.

8. Their Creation—Garden of Eden stories help explain how an all-powerful God chose to create and then continue in a relationship with a morally inferior and brazenly weak human race.

9. These stories presented justification for a needed priesthood to mediate between God and a fallen humanity, with no further reference to a relationship between cultic practice and the activity of the Devil.

10. Old and New Testament teaching about the Devil and her activity is not uniform or complete. The being presented is

a composite figure without clearly defined characteristics, motivation, intention, etc.

11. The many depictions of the Devil cannot be harmonized.

12. In some Scripture, the Devil and God seem hardly to be eternal adversaries but unusually "close." The Devil is actually privy to divine counsels and inner workings.

13. In some Scripture, God may he said to tacitly give the Devil "orders" to inflict evil.

14. In other Scriptures, God seems to endorse the notion of "turning people over to the Devil."

15. In almost all Scripture, where God seems purposely to interact with humans, no account is ever presented of such an interaction containing the Devil.

16. With the rise of Apocalyptic Literature in the Intertestamental Period, the Devil reappeared as a significant player in theology, but his presence in New Testament literature is minor compared to his importance and status as claimed in later Christian history.

17. Both Jesus and Paul appear to use the term the Devil, or Satan, figuratively, not literally.

18. Paul declares that the world is in bondage to evil manifestations due to the actions of God, not those of the Devil.

19. Jesus never claims that his primary stumbling block, spiritual concern, or enemy is the Devil.

20. Jesus' trials were consistently framed as overcoming temptation, not battling an Evil One.

21. By the middle of the Third Century, Origen and other Universalists had declared that God would finally save the Devil.

22. This is a significant comment on how many Church Fathers interpreted the Bible.

23. The Devil reemerges to become a major ingredient in Western Theology.

24. Eastern Christianity did not accept all of Western Theology, and has been far less rigid in formulating its ideas about the place and status of the Devil. Universalism is a strong undercurrent in its thinking to this day.

25. I conclude this lengthy, but indispensable, essay with the following, more practicable comments about an Evil One.

26. Those offended by the notion of God creating and sustaining evil seem not to take umbrage at the idea of God creating and sustaining the Devil.

27. On a daily, practical level, belief in the Devil seems to make little difference for those espousing the existence of such a being.

28. Few persons believing in the Devil would affirm that evil and sinister behavior in persons is the result of diabolical power completely negating human freedom.

29. In point of fact, the most horrendous evils in history need no more to account for them than human acts, influence, and behavior.

30. To attribute such acts to the Devil is a way of excusing, diminishing, or "justifying" them, as not committed wholly and entirely by persons.

31. No human act could ever be shown conclusively to have been influenced by the Devil.

32. Most so-called "direct manifestations of the power of the Devil" are quite trivial and banal, and can be otherwise explained.

33. That Christians may "feel" better spiritually and psychologically by attributing all evil to the Devil, and not to God, is irrelevant theologically.

34. The use of the terms "Satan," "the Devil," et al., to indicate a non-literal personification of evil is completely acceptable to Christian theology.

The God Above The God Too Small

A n irreverent wag has stated that clearly no one understands
the Bible since a new translation of it appears every fortnight!
Surely a case can be made for this kind of thinking. Long before the
contemporary spate of translations, J. B. Phillips released, in 1958,
his complete *New Testament in Modern English*. It has served readers well, especially those in his homeland, the United Kingdom
and the Commonwealth of Nations. Phillips is quoted as saying
that when he handled the ancient texts, he felt as if he were dealing
with electricity. That reverential wonder and awe are apparent in
his presentation of an impressive dynamic equivalence.

J. B. Phillips also left a long shelf of books, many of which are
well worth perusal. Most are short, quick reads with useful points
throughout. One of his most popular works was titled, *Your God is
Too Small* (1953). In it he properly asks if the God believed in by
most people can actually handle all the problems of contemporary
society. He simultaneously wondered whether many others were
unbelievers because the God offered in religious communities was
shallow and impotent. Phillips countered all that with the bold
statement, "Your God is Too Small!"

Paul Tillich was making a somewhat different, but not unrelated point, when, in much of his writing he attempted to redefine God. The God "above" the traditionally understood God
had many new characteristics, which Tillich wrote about repeatedly. As with Phillips, his idea is apparent. We need new ways of

referring to, understanding, and experiencing God, to Tillich, the "God Above God."

He was a powerful influence in Christian theology for several decades. He was beyond gifted at creating terms and phrases which were memorable, powerful, and mesmerizing. "Ground of Being," "The Courage to Be," "The Eternal Now," "Ultimate Concern," "The New Being," are just a few of the brilliant verbal sensations which he offered to theology.

One suspects that Tillich's experience as a Chaplain on the Western Front in World War I, may have presented him with the strong image of the "ground" of being. Trenches filling with the dead, as young soldiers senselessly fought for a few yards of that ground, can hardly leave one's psyche.

Fortunately, his influence is waning considerably and Christians are discovering that they do not need dazzling new phrases and words—the Biblical terms work just fine.

But Tillich should mainly be criticized for the fact that in his entire system of thought, he actually has no need whatsoever for Jesus of Nazareth. Everything he wrote can be affirmed without any reference to a living, historical Jesus. (I believe Tillich was a full-blown Spinozan pantheist!)

Both Phillips and Tillich help here, and their contribution may be obvious. To believe, as I do, in ultimate universal salvation, one must indeed expand one's view of God. I affirm that any God who consigns millions to either eternal damnation or final annihilation is much too small. So, the God above that God must be introduced and believed in.

Likewise, anyone denying that God is both creator and sustainer of evil believes in a God too small. The God above that God must also be introduced and believed in. In a previous book I shared my understanding of the God of universal salvation. In this book I am introducing the God who creates and sustains both good and evil.

The study of language is a fascinating thing. Linguistic Analysis is a relatively new area within the millennia's old discipline called "Philosophy." In the last century, its most brilliant thinker was Ludwig Wittgenstein. He concluded that most "problems" in thought are really confusions in our use of language. He, though deceased in 1951, still dominates those studies in critical thinking.

J. B. Phillips and Paul Tillich gave new ideas and new linguistic terms to our theological endeavors. As Christians, we must decide if their words are useful and actually assist us in better understanding the God revealed in the Bible. Surely, gods can be much too small, and surely there is a God above all the small gods we humans imagine.

The writer of 1 Timothy 3:16 used some words that we can appropriate splendidly. He used them with reference to Jesus Christ but they are perfect for us at this point: "Great indeed is the mystery of Godliness." We affirm that even if all our ordinary human language fails in its incompleteness, there is a God above our words about God!

Genesis: It Was "Good"

It is apparent that every sentence written about The Problem of Evil relates directly or indirectly to God. Without either evil or God there is no Problem for anyone to deal with. But there is a God, and there is evil; the Problem does not go away.

Believers do find that in all considerations here, the "God of the Problem" remains relatively constant and permanent, as defined by essential historic Christian Theology. It may well be that the Problem exists because God is who he is believed to be. This means that for the gods of some religions, and plainly for atheists, there is no Problem of Evil as it has come to be known. Other theologies present a god who may not be omnipotent, and so she is in constant struggle with evil. The outcome of the cosmic battle is not at all certain. Such a view is contrary to all Christian thinking, of course.

And others have observed and lived in such a ruthless, hurtful world that they have plaintively asked if God is good, hiding behind a veil of evil, or if God is evil, hiding behind a veil of good. Without the God of our Judeo-Christian tradition, properly defined, one might well make a case for such sad, shocking points of view. In any case, and even with our precious theological heritage, the sheer raw data of existence is ambiguous enough as it relates to understanding God. This ambiguity remains, and becomes the essential Problem of Evil. If we redefined God, the concern could simply vanish.

Where did we get our ideas about both God and the world, ideas which have largely framed this Problem for us? Let us turn to the Book of Genesis to determine if some of that ancient material has predisposed us to think and interpret in ways which are illogical, unsubstantiated, or simply false. Let us see how ancient Hebrews dealt with The Problem of Evil.

Those comfortable with critical Biblical scholarship believe that the Book of Genesis is a product of ancient priests writing with very specific goals in mind. "Genesis" means the origin or the coming-into-being of something. These priests gave a religious interpretation of the origins of multiple things, from the cosmos itself to the human species, from animals to geographic place names.

My immediate concern is with the fact that these writers tell the story of the creation of the earth, and repeatedly describe it as "good" or "very good." The Hebrew term is used seven times in Genesis 1, and five times in Chapter 2. For exegetical studies, the word can be translated in more than one way, but the commonsensical English word "good" is acceptable to almost all Hebraicists. "Good" and "very good" mean basically exactly what they say, with no further elaboration indicated. God creates, declares it good, the story moves on.

If the Jewish priestly writers intend for us to believe that they had a direct revelation that, after the creation, God literally spoke, "It is good," we rightly have legitimate concern about the factuality of that claim. It would presuppose an indefensible and quite unnecessary view of "inspiration." On the other hand, they declare that God indeed said it, and they were satisfied to write down that she did. Surely these ancient people were as familiar as are we with this world and all its evil potentialities. Did they see nothing latent in the world before the Fall? We do!

Or, does "good" simply fulfill the priestly need to address the Fall? The pristine state existed, the first couple disobeyed God, and the world thereafter was filled with blessing and plague. The Story of the Fall can perfectly account for that, and give historical continuity to a chosen people and a chosen priesthood. The story of the earth's human history could not be told without a religiously-defined view of the origin of sin and God's response. The priestly scribes wrote it down.

In the next essays we will see that "good" cannot mean "perfect," and that it cannot preclude the environmental components that must not go unnoticed. "Good" in these verses clearly does not preclude evil. It appears that when God says, "Good," it does not mean the complete absence of what we would define as both evil and sin. But God's relationship with evil begins long before the creation, as we shall plainly see.

Genesis: Evil Before The Creation

In the last essay I attempted to demonstrate that the ancient writers did not describe a creation which could not conceivably include evil. In fact, I will now make the case that in every Genesis 1 verse using the word "good," reference is being made only to what God has just created. Genesis 1:31 is the summary verse where the writers state that, "God saw everything he had made, and behold, it was very good." Everything created in the "six days" was pleasing to its Creator. But were there beings and entities, soon to be present in that creation, who were not created in those "six days," beings that had an existence ages before? It seems so. Perhaps God chose not to "see" everything that could be seen! Only what she saw was "good."

Everyone denying that God is the creator of evil must posit the existence of some other "creator of evil." Many Christians maintain that the culprit creator of all of our maladies is none other than Satan, the Devil, the Tempter, the Evil One, or the Old Deluder, as he has been variously named. This supernatural being, not the holy God, is the sure and certain cause of all evil. Even if God allows evil, as she clearly does, we must look away from her for its primal origination.

It may then logically be asked where this Satan came from. And many declare that to correctly answer we must go very far back into God's eternity, before the creation of the cosmos. There, they say, a monumental Battle in Heaven occurred, an event that would change everything for God and his creation.

There are obscure Bible verses which are mentioned in this regard. Isaiah 14:12, Daniel 12:1, and Job 1:6 are pieced together, giving a very sketchy outline of some aspects of these impenetrable events. The stories thereafter constructed are varied and somewhat confusing. Creating a timetable is impossible, but not really important, for the main points present themselves rather easily. Essentially, the drama is that in heaven, Satan, a beloved angel, rebelled against God, was cast out, and in an unclear sequence, was given (by God) the earth for his diabolical playground. That must be the case, we are told, for the same Satan suddenly discloses his presence on the newly-created earth and in the pristine Garden of Eden.

Does this clarify anything, or does it complicate our theology even more? It certainly raises a series of unsettling questions. For starters, what was abroad in the pre-creation "heaven" of God that would lead anyone to desire to rebel against God? How could even an angel "get the idea" to attempt a radical usurpation of heavenly power? More questions: Why does God allow all this to fester and erupt, finally leading to such catastrophic conclusions? There must have been something troubling about the eternal environment which fostered that temptation, outright revolt, and spurning of the laws of God. Furthermore, and finally, why did God not stop the insurrection? She obviously permitted it, with banishment as the divine solution.

In the end, the now-fallen angel was eventually allowed to "land" somewhere else, continuing her mischievous ways. As we know, this Satan landed on the good earth where his eyes must have glowed as they beheld "easy pickings" among God's newly-minted man and woman.

It is patently clear that nothing in the several variations of this fascinating myth satisfies any serious theological question about the origins of evil. Sadly for God, everything must point back directly to God's omniresponsibility. If God "allows" (the favorite term here) open rebellion, followed by a casting out, nothing is decided except that every vector points back to God the Creator.

(An interesting aside is the question: if God allowed this before Creation, could it happen again in the coming eternity?)

Most Bible students understand that conjecturing about much of this is based upon no Scriptural warrant whatsoever. These myths arise because our forebears asked the same questions we ask today. Our modern inquiries are no more articulate and learned than were theirs. The plots of ancient stories may not convince, but the residual ingredients are very familiar: God is responsible for evil, but we creatures must respond to it until God eradicates it eternally. We are hopelessly entangled with God in this our human plight. We see that we and writers of very olden times are spiritual contemporaries after all.

Genesis: The Garden

We now have Satan successfully cast out of heaven coming to dwell, unfortunately, on the earth, where he seems permanently ensconced. If God is active in this new Creation, so is Satan. (Many believe that he continues his devilish work into the present hour, with God completely aware of all his schemes.) The divine role in evil continues, even if puzzlingly defined.

I have stated that the Problem of Evil would perhaps not have its longstanding theological focus and power had ancient Hebrew writers not quoted God repeatedly in Genesis 1 and 2: "It is good or very good." The goodness of God reflected in the goodness of the Creation has been passionately defended by those who desperately attempt to show that the contaminating factor in Paradise was not God; it was none other than the fallen one, Satan. In this view, however, the "defense" of God breaks down, for God knows full well what is afoot, but merely observes until he judges the unhappy couple.

This is the exact duplicate of what has been reported about Satan's rebellion in heaven, eons past. God did not prevent that insurrection, and acted decisively only after it occurred. Here, God watches the interaction between Satan and the first couple, acting only to discover their "crime," and to announce the calamitous sentence for it. But Adam and Eve are not alone in "paying" for their wrongdoing: the cosmos itself, and every living thing, are enchained for all time.

Perhaps unwittingly the ancient scribes have described a newly-created world that was indeed "good", it was ironically now "good for Satan." In it, he could practice and display all of his most persuasive wiles without heavenly restraint. It can readily be seen that God's "very good" Creation was not at all crafted to bar or to prevent evil, sin, or eventually, death. Perhaps the Great Disruption of the Fall was not so cataclysmic as it was entirely predictable and expected under such circumstances. Adam and Eve had very little chance of *not* succumbing to the Evil One!

In their written reporting the Hebrew scribes had also used the phrase, "not good" (Gen 2:18). God saw that it was not good for the man to be alone. But as the story plays out, Adam was never alone. Of course he had a menagerie of animals, named by himself. He also had, lurking in his Garden, the Devil himself.

We have reviewed the outcomes of this building narrative. The supramundane creature encouraged lying, deceit, and treachery, even before the first bite of forbidden fruit. In myth or reality Adam and Eve are accounted the originators of sin. Sin perhaps, humanly speaking, but they did not originate the vast forces of malevolence arrayed against them, before which they would understandably capitulate, even before committing what history has erroneously labelled, "the first sin." I am assuming, of course, that the Devil can sin against God!

Genesis: The Proleptic Tree

A s we continue to analyze the things that lead humanity into the degradation of sin forever, the study of "nature" in the Garden is quite worthwhile. We discover that nature was neither friendly nor cooperative. Despite being labelled "good," it was, in reality, deadly.

God talks of nature in a speech which warns that there is a Tree from which the first couple should not eat. If they do they will surely "die." Adam and Eve can have no idea of what that actually means, and they consequently seem oblivious to the divine caution. Curiously, God does not mention what might well deserve another cautionary word: there is also a death-dealing and subtle serpent slithering through the Paradisal Garden. He will soon be using the fruit of nature as a killing instrument in his demonic strategy.

The unfolding drama swirls around the very strange Tree of the Knowledge of Good and Evil. The serpent, Satan, says you will not die if you eat its fruit; besides that, you will become like God, knowing good and evil. He successfully messages that the fruit is tasty, it is not deadly, and they will obtain a profound new understanding of many things. They eat, God finds out, and utters that the couple have become "like us." A shocked and dazed Adam and Eve are forced out of the Garden, the earth is cursed, Satan is cursed, and misery will follow all persons for all of human history. So goes the story.

I have no interest in literalizing anything in the narrative, but I repeat that the theological issues presented in these texts are hugely significant. They compel us to continue our reflections on God's involvement in the existence of evil.

We are comfortable with our holy God having "knowledge" of all good things, but these Scriptures teach that God is also familiar with all things evil. The mysterious tree is introduced as a kind of "divine repository" for God's knowledge of both. It is placed on the earth before Adam's fall. In the Tree, evil is present in an anticipatory way: if Adam eats, it will miraculously find a limitless source of dispersing power, burst forth, and spread its tentacles over all persons and all creation. Unknown to himself, Adam carries the "open sesame" key to the world's misfortune.

God knows all about evil, and exactly what will transpire if Adam eats the fruit. The world of thistles, hard work, sweat, difficult childbirth, curses and more, are all in God's prescription for this rash disobedience.

I have used the word "proleptic" to title this essay. It is a helpful term in Biblical studies, though rarely seen or used. Proleptic is an adjective which refers to a future event presumed to have already occurred. It allows the mingling of present and future, and is anticipatory of the future reality of what is envisioned. In these Genesis verses it can refer to "the mind of God" foreshadowing what Adam would do, including the results which would follow.

Biblical examples of prolepsis are quite numerous. God tells Abraham that he will be the father of many nations. God sees the future as living reality. The Apostle Paul declares his Universalist faith that in Christ all are made righteous. He sees it as if it is so.

In Romans 4:17, Paul uses these clarifying words: God calls things "that are not as if they were." That is a good definition.

Prolepsis should be differentiated from prophecy, but the two are related. Prolepsis is, however, contextually unlike prophecy, which is an announcement by God's living spokesperson that a definable event is "coming." (Prolepsis, prophecy, and predestination is a topic unrelated to this study.)

The Tree of the Knowledge of Good and Evil is the focal point, "ground zero," for what was in the mind of God, now becoming living reality. Who, then, created the evil outcomes which were visited upon the earth and all its creatures thereafter? Adam and Eve did not. Satan did not. God did.

This Genesis narrative is quite revelatory. Its literal reality or mythological status is quite irrelevant. The ancient Hebrew priests wrote a story rife with theological content which we must confront and acknowledge. They claimed much about God, and they clearly did not shirk to say that God created both good and evil. When Adam and Eve sinned, God called the world's evil into existence. So it was not in the Garden of Eden that God foresaw the coming ravages of the Fall. We Christians must come to peace with the fact that it was in the divine eternity. Genesis 1 and 2 give us little clarity; they take us into great mystery.

Could it be that the words in Genesis 3:22 are proleptic for all future generations who struggle with The Problems of Evil: "See, The Man has become like us, knowing good and evil!"? The Tree is good; why is it also evil? The world is good; why is it also filled with evil?

Genesis: The Smallest Things

Since the Book of Genesis was written in a "pre-scientific" age, we would not expect to read in the ancient text about certain kinds of life forms. As Christians, however, we affirm that God created everything that was, and is, part of this stunningly diverse planet. In our more modern era, we have the capability to explore much of God's handiwork, from the largest to the smallest.

I have spent a great deal of time, and many pages, making several key points. Among other things, I have said that God created evil and that the world contains vast potential for overwhelming evil. It is certain that great evil can emerge from the smallest places.

In discussions with atheist scientists about cosmic beginnings, Christian creationists believe they have the upper hand. As I stated earlier, part of their winning strategy is to demand answers to questions about "purpose" and "origins." But I trust that I have also shown that those questions are not answered with data which necessarily commends belief in the Christian God. Evil and its numerous manifestations present problems enough for believers, much less for non-believers. This essay adds another dimension to those considerations.

I am confessionally a believer, but I am not particularly interested in finding creation "science" and origins in an ancient book like Genesis. It is easy to acknowledge that the Scripture writers were attributing to God the entirety of creation, and were praiseful in so doing. I find that to be meaning enough in this early account.

I read those chapters and agree that there is indeed a marvelous creator God, but I have believed that quite independent of these early Hebrew verses. I ask no more of this first book of the Bible.

Christian apologists spend an inordinate amount of their time on this Book of Genesis and its account of the macro- or mega-creation: heaven, earth, planets, stars, sun, moon, and billions of galaxies. They will occasionally descend to consider the lower levels of biology and, for example, focus on the amazing brilliance of the function of the eye. They assert that this organ could not be the product of any known evolutionary process. That is well and good, but Christian defenders must go much, much deeper into nature and its component "parts."

Scores of particle physicists study phenomena which exist at the subatomic level. "Atom-splitting" is a familiar term, and research deriving therefrom is quite astounding. Scientists analyzing these results are confidently stating that they offer significant implications for understanding the grandest, most fundamental laws of nature, all the way to the laws of the structure of the entire universe. From the subatomic to the whole sweep of the cosmos is most impressive, even breathtaking!

Many true believers are scientists who also study subatomic particles. They claim that, in their faith opinion, the research points straight to a creator God. There are, however, other "small things" to be studied and commented upon by these Christian professionals. Do they also point to a loving God?

I am referring to the world of microbes, bacteria and virus, which can kill an individual person or tens of thousands. The plasmodium parasite is spread by mosquito bite, and causes malaria. That disease is, arguably, the greatest killer in all of human history. An HINI influenza A virus caused the so-called "Spanish Influenza" which took more lives than the nearly contemporaneous World War I.

I will refrain from further listing the dozens of other "creations" which can and have led to the same catastrophic and tragic outcomes for people and nations. Animals, too, are subject to such afflictions. The diseases, maladies, outbreaks, and epidemics have familiar names, known to all literate persons. The theological point is troublingly significant.

I am aware that an explanatory response has been given referencing many forms of present evil, apparently including microbes, virus and bacteria. The notion is that these entities arose after Adam was expelled from Eden and literally everything was cursed by God (Gen 3). This curse, not an act of creation by God, empowered the rise of this species of life.

This reasoning reminds instantly of the supposition presented by Charles Darwin, the father of a completely godless evolution. He envisioned that a fortunate combination of matter may have suddenly sprung to life, on a very remarkable primordial day, untold millions of years gone by! I think these two "explanations" are mirror images, not at all convincing.

Some Christians believe in a limited, divinely guided evolution which accounts for much of this large and small creation. But that view avoids nothing and inherits the same problems in any event. A God overseeing an evolution which eventually spawns these killer microbes is a God who presents all the many difficult questions addressed in this book.

We Christians simply have to admit, even if theologically reluctant, that the existence of such deadly "small things" is part of the mysterious working of our creator God. It is urgently incumbent upon creation scientists to move beyond argumentation and discussion of such things as the Six-Day Creation, the Age of the Earth, Noahic Floods, geological formations, and fossil findings. Those topics are surely interesting and exciting. But under the lens of a simple microscope lies a landscape with much to dazzle, amaze, and wonder about, in both dread and awe. There is, indeed, another world entirely, quite unknown and unimagined by ancient, priestly scribes. But it is God's world—and ours—finite, fascinating, fragile, and even frightening.

Noah And The Lost World

In this book I spend very little time dealing with the origin of evil in the "mind of God." The reason is simple. We can have no access to the actions, dreams, and plans of the Trinity prior to the creation of this cosmos. There is no revelation about such things. Someone unknown to me stated that there is a cross in the heart of God. That appears to be true, but no human being has the capacity to plumb the depths of such a profundity. The counsels of eternity are not our jurisdiction.

Nevertheless, I believe that the subject of origins is freighted with conclusions and implications that inescapably end in the same place: God is ultimately responsible for creating, sustaining, and finally ending all that is, including evil. Though unclear from our human perspective, God lovingly acts in every case, according to his "good pleasure." This divine omniresponsibility need not be avoided, even if it leads believers into the darkest mysteries of their lives of faith. Even as we stare questioningly into that infinity, or strain to peer into the "glass darkly" (1 Cor 13:12), we understand that in that very act itself, we are sustained and embraced by the God who loves us. So even without clear and satisfactory answers and details on the origin of evil, we can turn to other related matters.

The story of Noah is recounted in Genesis 5–9. It is filled with interesting themes and subjects, though most commentators do not go there for issues related to the Problems of Evil. I think those issues simply cannot be avoided.

What is God's motivation for flooding the earth and destroying humanity? In Genesis 6:5 and 8:21, God determines that "the inclination and imagination of the heart is only evil all the time, even from childhood." In chapter 6, God destroys the earth because of this human tendency and its accompanying evil, sinful actions. In chapter 8 she declares that she will never do that again, even though the evil inclination is apparently still there in the race. The flood did nothing to change human nature. How long would it be before God could make the exact same assessment of the flood-free world and its new sinful inhabitants!

Jewish theologians, in particular, have produced a rather large literature on this yetzer hara, the inherent human tendency to do evil. Their conclusions are that humans will inevitably sin, and are alone responsible for their own acts. Those sins are not compelled, nor can they be blamed on an outside entity. This diagnosis of the human condition becomes a helpful one when Temptation is discussed in a later essay.

Christian theology has waffled to and fro on this issue. Some have a very high opinion of innate human "goodness." They have literally run from a rather vacant term eagerly embraced by others: "total depravity." But "total" is a useless word, for nothing is one-hundred percent depraved or diseased, to use a medical analogy. There must be a presupposition that something "well" was there before the depravity advanced.

It is nonsense to point to the unredeemed race and declare them all completely and totally sinful. Common sense and the Bible note the large amount of good done by non-believers. God's prevenient grace extends to all persons everywhere. All manifestations of good must be referred to God. To do otherwise is a sin, for it takes glory from God.

Noah's story brings up the idea of instrumental evil. God destroys everything in order to punish sin and evil, and to accomplish ultimate good. But drowned in the waters are all animals and infants and babes in the womb. They are accounted in the churning flotsam. The fresh start is sweeping and all- inclusive, but it is built on a terrible carnage.

Was the calamity evil, even if it was done for other reasons, which supposedly were entirely satisfactory to God? The world was remade only after the unfolding of unimagined horror, panic, and ultimate death. The story is a perfect example of the loving God creating an inordinate amount of pain and death, exacting it on humans, animals, and the earth itself.

As in every catastrophe of any kind, people of flesh and blood "come out of it," but with indelible physical, psychological, and spiritual scars. Noah and his family survived, but as the water subsided and the earth dried, this man showed many behaviors for which the destruction had originally come. Soon enough, he showed his common humanity, and the sinful race began again.

I could, of course, write many similar chapters on peoples and individuals, Biblical and non- Biblical, who lived through unthinkable situations. The facts would change, but the analyses would not. Human to human struggles are one thing. Calamity and tragedy visited from God are another. Regardless of who or what "caused" the flood, real people had to deal with it. The story is, therefore, not only about Noah and his small family.

I leave Noah to his new world and his energy to start afresh. I leave him with his memories. I cannot, however, end this as did Camus: and we must think of him happy!

Theological Interlude

In this essay I will make two significant points that I believe work as a bridge between Old Testament ideas and those found in the New Testament. One is the sudden disappearance, in the Old Testament, of the Devil, or Satan, as the instigator of evil and its many manifestations. The second is the Pauline view of the world and the cosmos, as he forcefully describes it in the Book of Romans.

The Devil's role as key player in the introduction and continuation of evil is diminished exponentially with God's curse in Genesis 3:14. Apparently the Evil One goes from standing upright to crawling on his "belly," and essentially slithers off the stage of the Old Testament. He makes cameo appearances here and there, and has a major role in the Book of Job. Even there, however, he is initially cozy in heaven with God and asks if he can perpetrate evil on a good man. He is given permission so to do. He is God's instrument in inflicting horrendous pain, suffering, and loss on hapless people and animals. God observes the testing; Job remains faithful; the Devil disappears into other dimensions.

The Old Testament is filled with calamity, from beginning to end. What is important here is the reminder that God is the initiator of much of it. God "creates" evil in story after story and situation after situation. The ancient writers struggle with this fact, since they are convinced of their "chosen people" status. Even so, they often accept their fate, affirming that unfaithfulness has led God to inflict evil in order to then bless and redeem. The flouting of law and righteousness invites divine wrath, which often leads to humble obeisance in the fear of God. The cycle is endless. The ancients recognize quite well that evil crushes both the "good and the bad" indiscriminately. They can only lament and watch history play out.

The Old Deluder does reemerge in New Testament literature, and is in some texts claimed to have enormous power, but in others not so much. Generally, those twenty-seven books take little notice of an Evil One who may match God's goodness with an equal amount of evil. Listing the verses in which he appears is instructive, but no consistent portrait of him or his activity is apparent or possible to describe.

Next, we look to the Apostle Paul who makes some quite noticeable comments about the cosmos. It must be remembered that Paul was a Jew, a Pharisee, and had studied at the feet of Gamaliel. We might use anachronistic language and label him a Ph. D. scholar in Old Testament studies. We do well to take note of how he viewed the status of the cosmos vis-a-vis its pervasive evil components. Of course, he was completely familiar with the Genesis accounts of the "good" earth being suddenly transformed in the Garden of Eden stories.

The Book of Romans is an unsystematic assemblage of Pauline teaching. He travels far and wide in the early chapters, which culminate in the rhapsodic announcement of Universal redemption in chapter 11. He had earlier made several statements about the ultimate salvation of all, but is emphatic here. In chapter 12 he moves into more ethical, less theological teachings. Despite its darting indirection, it is the greatest work of Christian theology ever penned.

Paul does comment on the state of the cosmos, and his words are ominous. In chapter eight he is apparently referencing the world after the Fall and God's curse. This language is crisp and intentional. The good creation is now "anxiously longing, waiting, subjected to futility, groaning, suffering as a woman in the pains of childbirth" (vs. 19–22). How could this be? How could it happen to the "very good" creation of Genesis? Who, indeed, has "subjected" the earth to this disastrous fate? Paul is very clear: this did not happen to the creation "willingly", the Lord God subjected it to all these things (v. 20).

Paul's use of the word "willingly" is strange and odd. He is using anthropomorphic language throughout, of course. The creation itself has no volition to make such a choice, but his word does underscore that the current subjection is unnatural, given the original status. Paul next adds that the creation is "waiting eagerly" for something dramatic: "the revealing of the sons of God" (v. 19). We are almost clueless as to what the Apostle had in mind in using this phrase, and every answer is speculative. The cosmos is in these chains of bondage until something happens; we might ordinarily offer that the freeing will occur at the End of Time. Paul could have written that; he did not. Certainly, however, we can understand Paul to mean that if God subjected the cosmos to these realities, God herself will be the sole agent to "free" it.

In Romans Paul makes a substantial advance upon Old Testament Theology. In the Jewish scriptures, it was never quite stated that the plight of the world is the direct result of the action of God. Paul says it plainly.

The Apostle moves off the subject quickly, however, without enumerating all the implications he sees from this pronouncement. We would like more information here, but do not have it. Paul, as a good Jew, does not teach that because of the state of the world, the human race has "no chance," but is completely at the mercy of powers of evil. Certainly, Jewish theology would allow no one to say that their sin was "caused" by outside influences, however strong. We think of Adam and Eve as almost incapable of resisting evil. We cannot think that way about any of God's children thereafter. Paul would say that sin is volitional and a violation of the law of God. He would spend little time reflecting on "the social causes" of sin, despite his fervent belief in such transpersonal and supermundane entities as "principalities and powers."

With these brief comments we see that Paul has reframed the entire situation. As we turn to the life of Jesus, we must remember that, if Paul is correct, the Savior lives his few years in a world enchained in spiritual bondage—by God.

Jesus And The Problems Of Evil

Surely in the life and teachings of Jesus we have answers to our deepest questions about evil and sin. There is good news and not so good. Jesus addresses some of our concerns, but this is beyond true: Jesus did not come to "solve" the Problem of Evil.

Greek, Roman, and Jewish thinkers were vexed by this Problem. It was natural that Christians inherited it, now to be viewed through their new perspectives on the Incarnation. Did this aid them in grappling with the troubling issue of a now newly-defined God and her involvement in evil? In the next three essays we will see that, on the contrary, it may have forever compounded the Problem!

We note once again that even when we look to Jesus, the issue must be understood as one about the very being, nature, and activity of God. The title of a book of essays by C. S. Lewis is *God in the Dock*. The image is of God appearing as a witness in a courtroom. Most of us wince at the thought of sinful humanity arrogating to itself such a prerogative as to quiz God about anything much. But the image is very honest, in fact. Who has not been passionately desirous of answers, clarifications, and interpretations of many events occurring in their lives or the lives of others. And who alone has the answers, but God.

But if we do not have public access to our God, we do have Jesus, and we have many details about him. Yet, we are stopped in our tracks when we discover that Jesus asks the same questions we do! If indeed God is good, "My God, my God, why have you forsaken me?"

I will point to a few things Jesus does help us with, however. He acknowledges that, for example, people are born blind, become lame, develop incurable gynecological maladies. He notes that children are plagued by epilepsy, and adults by mental illness, including, we assume, schizophrenia. He is aware that buildings fall, taking human life, and that wind and wave can sink boats. People suffer from leprosy and present great physical incapacities. He observes that birds die in midair and plummet to earth.

Jesus is keenly and compassionately aware of the significant place of all these manifestations of evil in the world. What is his "explanation?" In truth, he offers none, but leaves us firmly on the horns of the dilemma: God is loving and good, and completely in charge of a world full of marvelous things, but just as full of pervasive, sometimes overwhelming evil. But we also come away with the transparent fact that Jesus lives his life in the same earth—bound context as do we. He knows well that eventually, through a confluence of much of this evil, he will die. He does not withhold from his followers: absent some cataclysmic ending, a "Second Coming," death is inevitable for all.

Jesus does teach extensively about corporate sin and evil, those institutionalized realities that are beyond the creation or culpability of one person, or even thousands. These are the entities which can be referred to as "principalities and powers," and they exist in both high and low places. Jesus knows this very well.

He understands that Roman government and law provide and maintain social structure and a semblance of peace. But it also oppresses and punishes without remorse. He was not unaware of its propensity—he will learn it well—to execute the innocent along with the guilty. This Roman presence gave excuse for the activity of politically dissatisfied rioters and insurrectionists. Jesus may actually have had such firebrand persons in his entourage of twelve disciples. Some of these malcontents reacted to Roman rule with intense hatred, violence, even murder.

Jesus also knew that his Jewish religious tradition could be an evil impersonal power to be reckoned with. It could both communicate God's grace, and squelch it mercilessly with its hidebound recalcitrance. Priests at the house of God might exact exorbitant fees for exchanging money and selling living sacrificial offerings. For the sake of an ancient command, religious leaders stiffened the spine to walk right past a battered, bloody human being on the side of the road. Animals could be left to languish and suffer in a ditch due to a Sabbath day proscription.

He bristled as he commented further. Pharisees could well bless the populace and have nothing to do with the needy or outcast. Sadducees were after worldly comfort at the expense of any and everyone. These Jewish traditions could ensure the lifelong economic and sexual exploitation of women, as such persons, in theory, could be handed from one sibling to another, confirming their status as "property."

Jesus basked in the light of Roman governmental freedom and security, at least for a time. He prized and enjoyed his true Jewish heritage as a gift from God. But he chastised and criticized both Roman and Jewish leaders, at times mincing no words. But he did not offer grand schemes for social restructuring, nor propose laws ensuring equality and justice. He had another agenda entirely.

He leaves us humanly situated in a corrupt, fallen world, where mighty powers and forces can produce unimagined good, but also catastrophic and crushing evil. Perhaps he meant us to ponder long and hard on things like these: the poor you always have with you, and there will always be wars and rumors of wars. He implied that sin, evil, and corruption little change, century after century. We are wise enough to finish Jesus' sentence: "You will always have with you . . . ." The list is painfully long.

Was Jesus simply a sad, negative, "doom and gloom" preacher? Not at all! If he did not speak to many other things, he did speak to this: the world is fallen, but people can change through grace! He was very specific in what he said he had come to "seek and to save", sinners (Mark 2:17; Luke 5:32). We may wish he had come to do many other things, but he did not. It seems that doing these other things is up to us.

How, then, does Jesus help us in dealing with our ordinary human sinfulness, defined as willful disobedience to the revealed commandments of God? Jesus brings us two things: his teachings and his life. With his teaching he sets us on the road to salvation, and by giving up his life, he assures that salvation for us.

Examination of the person and work of Jesus is a topic far outside the scope of this book. (I hope to address that soon in another place.) The following two essays go more deeply into some important aspects of the interchange between the Nazarene and ever-present evil.

Jesus And Impending Evil

There have always been Christian thinkers who have said something like this: "If you want to know what God thinks and how God acts, just look at Jesus of Nazareth." That idea is based upon a theology of incarnation in which the eternal God has taken on flesh as God-The-Son. God in Christ will essentially imitate God in heaven. Those comparisons and summations seem obvious on the surface, but must be used with appropriate caution.

For example, Jesus himself declares his own limitations in several life areas, which are not God's limitations. In the dread-filled Garden of Gethsemane, he openly states that his will does not parallel the Father's will. Many other examples could be given, enough to conclude that determining whether Jesus is "thinking and doing" what God would do is a matter of careful contextual exegesis. Equating Jesus' response with God's response is usually safe enough, but the exceptions must be noted.

There are numerous incidents in the synoptic gospels in which we are able, through what Jesus does and says, to gauge God's response to manifestations of evil. I am quite sure that these verses reinforce the positions I am taking in this book. They are perfectly clear "Bible" examples or situations in which believers could desperately and painfully ask: "If God is loving, why this impending evil? If God is immanently near—in this moment— why does she not act to help or to save?" On a very few occasions Jesus actually deals with these questions, and those incidents must be investigated with wondering concern. The stories I will examine are these: the disciples in a storm at sea, and John the Baptist in prison.

In Matthew 8, Mark 4, and Luke 8, a story is told of disciples at sea, Jesus asleep in the boat's stern, and a fierce, sudden storm. Each gospel writer used similar sources, added editorially, but presented the essential and equivalent scene. With Jesus sleeping soundly, the boat is being swamped, in clear danger of sinking. Finally, the frantic disciples wake him, and in Matthew and Luke say, "We are perishing!" Mark pens a more direct confrontation with the drowsy Jesus. The panicked disciples protest: "Do you not care that we are perishing?" And with that they have asked the ancient, universal question of all the Problems of Evil. One powerful enough to calm a raging sea lies in restful sleep a few feet away, but is seemingly oblivious to their desperate plight.

The questions of whether the disciples believed Jesus had any power over the raging waves, or whether they simply needed help with the oars and navigation, are irrelevant. Something far more profound is being addressed in this pericope. To the great relief of the passengers, Jesus happily awakes, and calms and stills the storm. But then inexplicably he chides his simple followers: "Why are you afraid? Where is your faith?" Even latter-day believers brace at that question!

"Carest thou not that we perish?" is from the King James version, and also appears in an old, old hymn. It is the legitimate question. The answer: "Why are you afraid and demonstrating such miniscule faith?" The Bible says that the disciples marveled at Jesus' power over a roiling nature. We may marvel at other things: Is fear and dread in the face of impending evil and potential death truly a lack of faith? And the most blatantly obvious point is simply that untold numbers of human souls, in peril on land and sea, likewise pray for help, but are not rescued—even while the Almighty God is very near. This is a story straight from Holy Writ perfectly illustrating the deep mystery of the larger Problem of Evil. There is another.

John the Baptist had every right to make inquiries about the man Jesus. After all, he was now languishing away in a prison under the control of the sadistic Herod Antipas. Luke's apparently independent source relates that John had perhaps impulsively rebuked Herod about his marital situation and was consequently shut up in prison. Both Matthew and Luke tell of John's plaintive inquiry of Jesus: "Are you the one who is to come, or are we to wait for another?" (Matt 11:3; Luke 7:19).

We cannot be sure of everything John is asking here, but it seems transparent that he is wondering if he has properly aligned himself, or touted and promoted the wrong "Messiah." We can wonder why John is not asking for an intervention of some kind that might facilitate his release from what must have been a nightmare environment.

We assume that the prison was hellish enough and that John may well have had more on his mind than just considering things about Jesus. Surely John pondered if his very life were hanging by a thread. In actuality, it was. Jesus, no doubt, was not unfamiliar with potential outcomes from an incarceration under the brutal Herod. These, then, seem to be the existential issues.

Nevertheless, Jesus' "reassurance" to John leaves us quite puzzled: "Tell John what you have seen." Is this reminder enough for John to understand that he was right to side with Jesus? Could this pacify and calm the inquiring preacher? But then the next words from Jesus may have baffled John, as they have all who have reflected on the Problems of Evil. Jesus instructs the messengers to say to John: "Blessed is anyone who takes no offense at me." And the ambiguity of this verse has haunted interpreters since it was spoken.

I have no particular interest in a purely exegetical investigation into Jesus' words. My concern is to state this: a man is in severe crisis—even unto death—and the Son of God says, "Do not be offended!" The verse is in complete concert with all theological and philosophical answers ever given to the perennial question: "If God is good, why is there evil—so much evil?" There is no direct or satisfying answer ever!

And yet the words possess a priceless spiritual dimension, which must not be overlooked in our chagrin or unsettledness. "Do not be offended in me," is not completely dismissive or cheaply callous. Rather, it communicates almost tender understanding and deep concern over the plight of the beloved John. And if for John, so for all believers. Perhaps it is a true glimpse of the heart of Jesus.

Perhaps it is an eschatological reference communicating: "Maintain trust, faith, hope, and do not be offended into despair and disbelief. You will be blessed eventually." Perhaps.

If Jesus sometimes says exactly what God would say, this appears to be one of those unfathomable, mysterious times. In this case, impending evil will lead to a horrific, senseless beheading. Supposing Jesus could not know that, he well knew something ominous was near to hand. Still, "Tell John not to be offended."

God is speaking here, I am very confident. Our spiritual challenge is to look squarely at the evil all around, but not take offense at the God we serve. On the Cross of Calvary, Jesus will struggle to decide whether to take offense at the God who sends him there. Thankfully for Christians, we know the outcome.

Jesus And The Great Mystery

I have made the point that Jesus' life, work, and teaching do not "solve" the Problem of Evil. In this essay I will affirm that, on the contrary, Jesus' life and ultimate death present data which monumentally compounds the Problem. It does so because Jesus is completely certain that his suffering and death occur as the direct result of the activity of his God. There are moments of ecstatic intimacy with his Father; there are moments of profound spiritual and physical agony. For Jesus, God not only creates evil, but afflicts the Only Begotten Son from the beginning of his ministry to his ignominious death.

At the outset we note that the Master deals existentially with his God, not with Satan. I believe the case can be made (I will not do it here) that Jesus' use of the term "Satan" or the "Devil" is always figurative, not literal. The stark reality is: Jesus does not need the Devil when he has his God!

A second point to be made here is to ask what is the origin of Jesus' self-identity. And all Bible students will agree that his self-reflections are almost always rooted in the Scriptures of the Old Testament. He focused on several terms and ideas from those ancient texts: "Lord," "son of man," "Messiah," "suffering servant." In those Scriptures there were conflicting definitions of some of those terms, however. Jesus eschewed any militaristic ideas of Messiahship. Notions of a powerful, conquering Coming One were prevalent in both Scripture and in first century thought. Jesus had to counter those beliefs and attempt to inform his Jewish neighbors that he understood the Messiah to be a Suffering Servant. Jesus' emphasis was on both words: suffering and servant. Unfortunately for him as a servant, he would truly suffer greatly at the hands of the Jewish and Roman populace. But he would suffer perhaps more acutely at the hands of his Abba, Father.

The texts which Jesus read in order to reach these clarifying conclusions about his life and work are the same ones we can read today. I will review only a few. There is no need to recount his life events, but only to present how he or the gospel writers interpreted some of those events.

Of course, everything begins at his baptism by John, where it was confirmed to him that he was the Beloved Son. After this exaltation he is driven into the wilderness, by God's own Spirit, to be tried by "the Devil" (Mark 1:12). This is the earliest clue that for Jesus the fundamental problem for himself and all humanity is not some evil supernatural being. It is temptation. His life, from this point until his death, can be analyzed in terms of his confrontation with, and overcoming of, the trials of temptation.

Perhaps Jesus was constantly thinking of the Suffering Servant Poems of Isaiah, but he may certainly have been doing so when he told his bewildered disciples, "I have a baptism to be baptized with, and how I am constrained until it is accomplished" (Luke 12:50). The verb tense is future; the constraint is the ominous sense of foreboding at the terrible burden he was constantly carrying. Though undefined and unknowable to Jesus, he knew that this second baptism will have no heavenly dove descending, or the voice of God triumphantly declaring him the Chosen One.

So, who will baptize him the second time? Not the greatest of all prophets, the strange John the Baptist. This time, God herself will immerse him in the deep, cold waters of suffering, pain, rejection, ridicule, and death. Is it possible that there will be a second exaltation, even after his death? Jesus has reason to believe it so.

The Messiah does not know all the details of his dying and death, but he takes charge of what he can, and deliberately orchestrates the confrontation which will lead to it. He, therefore, "sets his face steadfastly toward Jerusalem" (Luke 9:51). He had a rendezvous with religious leaders, Roman officials, the rabble, and a cohort of brutal, sadistic soldiers. He also had a rendezvous with God.

Jesus pays very little attention to most Old Testament teachings which could be applied to a future spiritual leader of Israel alone. He does, however, rely on a few selected texts which refer to a universal spiritual leader. He has always believed that God called the Nation of Israel to be a light to all peoples. Jesus personalizes that task and its demands as his very own.

The prophet Isaiah was Jesus' focal point for much self-understanding. He read Isaiah as if the words were directed exclusively to him. He would be the Universal Redeemer, but could accomplish this only by first being the Suffering Servant. It would all be the work of God, before, during, and after his own death. God would both inflict the suffering and declare him Savior. Afterward, he trusted, God would exalt him.

Jesus believed these related Isaiah passages were piercingly decisive: "We esteemed him stricken, smitten by God" (53:4); "God has laid on him the iniquity of us all" (53:6); "It was the will of God to bruise him. God has put him to grief" (53:10).

Jesus understands that God uses the instrumentality of religious leaders, scoffers, and soldiers. They are, oddly, carrying out the will of God. Jesus' cry at the end is a laser beam of his theology: My God, my God, why is this happening this way? But despite everything, to Jesus, God is his God. Of course, Jesus is here quoting Psalm 22, which begins with this agonizing question, but ends with such high note words as: all the earth shall praise God, even the one who could not keep himself alive (22:29). In his mortal flesh he cannot triumph nor be exalted. But God can make his death triumphant, and God can exalt the innocent one who is so wretchedly dying.

This message of redemption was not lost on the sadistically voyeuristic Jewish leaders standing near the cross. Their murderous chagrin must have been obvious to everyone when they heard him say, "Father, forgive them." But even worse to them, he added, "They do not know what they are doing"!!

We conclude these thoughts by reiterating that God creates evil, applies evil to his creatures and to his only Son, and then God "justifies" these mysterious happenings by and through things that occur after death. What happens at Calvary is the paradigm for this process: suffering, death, resurrection to glory. That seems to be the only answer to the profound "why?" of the Problems of Evil, which experientially involves us all, and most assuredly did the holy Son of God. His story is tragic, but it is, after all, our salvation.

Stephen, Paul, And Impending Evil

If two statements from Jesus help us learn of God's reaction to evil, so do the episodes of Stephen and Paul. In Jesus' words, we saw compassion and concern, mixed with ambiguity, from a God in very close proximity to saints in peril on the sea. We heard acknowledgement and empathic discernment, with the same ambiguity, from a God at some physical remove from John's dank and dark prison. In Acts and in 2 Corinthians we are confronted with similar messaging.

Early in the Acts of the Apostles we are introduced to a man "full of faith, the Holy Spirit, grace, and power" (Acts 6:5,8). Stephen was chosen by the apostles to distribute aid to some Hellenist widows. In the event he is brought before the "council" for preaching Jesus. When he appeared, his face was as "that of an angel" (6:15). That countenance would not help; forbidden to speak, he did not mince words. The longer he spoke the angrier became the crowd. Perhaps Stephen did as well, for by the end of the longest sermon recorded in Scripture, he unwisely attacks his auditors. In what are his concluding remarks, he gazes skyward and tells what he sees: a describable, visual revelation. "I see the heavens opened and Jesus standing at the right hand of God" (7:56). But Jesus is apparently merely observing. The audience had heard enough, and grinding their teeth, they rushed at him with one impulse, driving him out of the city. Waiting for no Roman authorization for an execution, they carry out a most painful and horrendous act. They stone poor Stephen. He is dead, the first martyr of the Christian Church.

It is obvious that Luke intends for the end of Stephen's life to remind his readers of the end of the life of Jesus. Similar and familiar words are used. Doubtless, too, Luke meant to convey that the epiphany of the Risen Lord was a source of great, abiding comfort to a man about to confront a ruthless death. But the heavenly response is another example of the heavenly beings observing great tragedy, suffering, and pain, and doing nothing to prevent it. The Triune God is passive as grisly events unfold, snatching the life from a man lauded with accolades and praise, precisely a person needed in the nascent Church. His talent went with him to an early death.

This is just the kind of situation which has been viscerally troubling to believers for many centuries. Christians can tolerate sin and evil proportionate to a basic understanding of overcoming both in order to grow in grace. It is overwhelming, senseless, irrational evil that disorients and disturbs. That is, of course, the essence of the Problems of Evil for Christianity. Perhaps in heaven, Jesus always stands when his precious saints are in trouble. If that is the celestial reaction, he will never sit!

I can be brief in dealing with the relevant story about the great apostle Paul. I am registering the same point about the perceived reaction of God to evil in the lives of real people. In 2 Corinthians 12, Paul's visit to the third heaven led God to "allow" Satan to send him a "thorn in the flesh." What exactly that was, we can only speculate. The significant part is that Paul is now afflicted by the very God who allowed him access to another world in the first place. Paul refers to Satan, but clearly places that being in the direct control of God. Paul has no "thorn" unless it is there by God's action. (Whether Paul actually believed in a Devil/Satan, with ontological status like into humans, is another topic.)

To be rid of this thorny hindrance Paul implores God three times. God's response is crucial to those addressing the Problems of Evil. A worthy man is seemingly in great distress, asks God for succor and relief, and God responds, "My grace is sufficient for you, for my power is perfected in weakness" (12:9).

It seems perfectly clear that the first part of the verse is "all" of the response that Christians will ever receive from the divine portals. "Why is there so much overwhelming, pervasive evil?" "My grace is sufficient for you!" If that means that we shall never have an answer in this world, and we shall not, we do have abundant "grace" to see us through. Grace reinforces faith, and though troubled and perplexed, we move on attempting faith-informed servanthood.

The second part of the verse offers more: "My power is perfected in weakness." Its incarnational allusion is transparently discernible. The Son of God conquers all evil through giving up power and opting for undeserved suffering. The Resurrection is God's affirmation of Jesus' choice to decline power and accept weakness and service.

The message for latter-day Christians is not entirely clear. As with many texts we grasp some of the inherent teaching, but confess that we cannot comprehend it all. What did Paul think this audible message meant? We cannot be sure. He was a self-sacrificing saint who gave up everything earthly to receive everything heavenly. He became the second most influential man in all of history. In 1 Corinthians he had confidently written, "Imitate me as I imitate Christ." Perhaps we can do that within obvious limits.

In view of our concerns with the manifestations of crushing evil, we have to work to determine the meaning of such verses for ourselves. "My grace is sufficient for you," presents some rich, unspeakable blessings, but also places barriers and limitations in front of our efforts. "My strength is made powerful in weakness" is a true paradox. Perhaps in following Jesus and Paul, we can learn its deeper meanings in gradual but personally discernible ways. I am quite sure that for many Christians and theologians, the Problems of Evil are a mountainous "thorn in the flesh." We sorely need this divine bestowal of grace.

The Hate Approved By God

In this book I have tried repeatedly to show the sheer magnitude of the philosophical and theological Problem of Evil. I have also attempted to demonstrate that a loving God is aware of the struggles of her children in dealing with the many aspects of the Problem. In this essay I will offer some comments on a strong human emotion, hate, and its relationship to both sin and evil.

The assumption can be safely made that all humans are capable of angry, hate-filled expressions in both word and deed. Good mental health counselors may ask the question of their clients: "What do you do with your anger?" It invites the counselee to admit the reality of his or her anger, and then to reflect on how that emotion manifests itself in daily life. Anger and hate are not equivalents, and obvious distinctions can be made.

Emotions reaching the level of hate are often difficult to control, sometimes leading to poor decisions and regrettable actions. The term "emotionally handicapped" is useful in describing the sad situation in which rational faculties and cognition give way to pure emotion. Much of self-control is thereby forfeited. (It would be a helpful and interesting Bible study to identify people and situations in which reason and faith completely succumbed to sheer emotional reaction.)

While growing up we all heard many things about hate. Family, friends, and clergy may have told us to "hate the sin but love the sinner." In that, they were surely right. We may also have heard that we "must not hate." In that, they were surely wrong, but with strong, Biblical caveats. There is a hate which is acceptable to God, and Christians are taught about it directly in Scripture.

The Greek word for hate is miseo. It has the equivalent meaning of the English word used to translate it: extreme visceral reaction, aversion, disdain. It moves emotion far beyond nonchalance and indifference, focusing it like a spotlight on the object of its concern. Since every emotion should have an object, what are Christ's followers to hate? And the text is very clear, as we shall see.

We need spend little time on the negative, sinful hatred we read about in the sacred writings. The object of that strongly condemned emotion may be many things: God, Christ, Israel, noblemen, enemies, the light, other persons, etc. The list goes on, detailing the morally unacceptable uses and expressions of hate. God calls such hate, "sin."

There are some other, quite interesting uses of the term, however. Jesus says there is a blessedness in being hated (Lk 6:22, for example). And Paul brings us back to hating the sin but not the sinner, when in Romans 7:15 he declares that he hates the sin he himself is committing.

The clearest teaching on the decisive difference between sin and sinner is given by Jesus Christ. It is, curiously, a strong commendation for hating, and thereby raises that emotion to a high status in all discussions of morals and ethics. Very little attention has been given to righteous indignation and hatred as God-given motivators for action against sin and evil. But, nevertheless, it has been before us in Holy Writ all the time.

In Revelation 1–3 the writers of the Johannine corpus picture Jesus talking about the Seven Churches of Asia. He is dissecting each one, making comments about both their righteous and unrighteous ways. In chapter 2 he is speaking to the church at Ephesus, and in 2:6 he states: "This is what you have in your favor: you hate the way of the Nicolaitans." Then the editors finish the sentence with these graphic and illuminating words: "which I also hate." Jesus hates, and the Ephesian Christians are saluted for hating—what? The sinful actions of the heretical Nicolaitans. We note again the crucial point that believers are not to hate the persons, but are definitely to hate the sin. Christians cannot hate people. It so happens that God loves them all!

Hearing and believing Bible verses does not automatically change one's life, thereby empowering all the actions enjoined in Holy Writ. Most Christians turn to the Word for its prohibition or blessing on behaviors and actions. Often overlooked is the fact that the Bible gives commandments for our emotional and affective lives. We are told both what to love and what to hate. Someone rightly said that we should study the text for many reasons, but one is certainly this: the Bible knows us very well.

I have affirmed that the Triune God commends and blesses some anger and hatred. I offer these comments in closing.

1. Jesus often shows great anger, which does not lead to sin.

2. The Book of Revelation says that Jesus actually hates sin.

3. Anger, even hatred, are divinely approved emotions in certain circumstances.

4. Both these affects can be strong motivators for action against sin and evil.

5. Christians must "rage against" certain evils. Indifference to the multiple manifestations of evil is condemned repeatedly in Scripture.

6. Both hatred and anger appear to originate as a concomitant part of the Problem of Evil.

7. Since God will resolve all the issues of the Problem in her eschatological age to come, it is certain that anger and hatred will be extinguished forever.

We are to love generously and hate sparingly. It is our job as believers to know the difference!

Temptation For Perfection

The writer of the Epistle of James was inexcusably wrong when he penned his several verses on temptation in chapter 1 (vss. 12–15). To his credit, however, he does not mention the Devil as an integral ingredient. God cannot be tempted by evil, which no one would dispute. Then he adds: and God himself does not tempt anyone.

In order to write that, he must have forgotten a great deal of what he should have known from the Old Testament: Abraham did not wonder who was commanding him to kill his son. (Gen 22:2). Job knew that behind the wiles of Satan was an empowering God (Job, passim).

And if James had any information about the earthly life of Jesus of Nazareth, he had radically reinterpreted many stories and events wherein Jesus was clearly being tempted by God. Jesus' ministry began with baptism, after which he was forced by the Spirit of God to be tempted in desert places. If the Spirit facilitates the tempting events, and God allows the Devil to be the tempting intermediary, what conclusions can be drawn? Jesus is also famously quoted as saying, "The Spirit is willing but the flesh is weak" (Matt 26:41). For most mere mortals, however, the opposite is true: the spirit is weak and the flesh is very strong. Some temptation is mental and spiritual, but most is "of the flesh."

In the so-called "Lord's Prayer," the words are addressed to God: "lead us not into temptation." Though we know them by heart and can speak them without thinking, they sound as if they convey the message that God has a great deal to do with this "leading" into temptation.

In the terror of the Garden of Gethsemane, Jesus is sorely tried, but prays, "not my will but thine" (Matt 26:39, et al.). This is a clear indicator that Jesus' will would have taken him out of this context, which was leading to his death. God's will was otherwise. On the cross of that death Jesus' cries to God are not anything if they are not the temptation to wonder where was his God, and why was she allowing this outrageous travesty to occur. From Gethsemane to the borrowed tomb, no supernatural "Evil One" is mentioned. The entire event is of and from God.

Furthermore, James posits that the locus of temptation is in the inner person: "Each one is tempted when he is carried away and enticed by his own lust" (1: 14). But Hebrews 4: 15 is plain: "Jesus was tempted in all the ways we are." Was Jesus being carried away and enticed by lust? Christians would do well not to attribute impure motives to the sinless Jesus. James does not help us here.

And we hasten to add that surely the Hebrews writer is correct: Jesus was tempted, and the verse is quite meaningless unless the Nazarene had the capacity to sin. The theological term is "peccable:" capable of sinning.

Why could James not see that temptation is composed of two obvious parts: the interior thought or "fantasy," coupled with some sort of exterior "tempter." For Jesus in the wilderness, the temptations were visual and verbal. He was presented with choices about which he could think, and visions which he could see: bread, pinnacles, kingdoms. Of course, he countered each with verses from Deuteronomy, words precious to Jews as verses of power when they, too, were wandering in the wilderness as a people of God. Jesus' words remind all believers of the great benefit of memorizing Scripture as life's battles are fought (Deut 11: 18, et al.).

We are inclined to think of temptation in terms of want and deprivation. We wish, we dream about, having more. Driving our wishes may be a sinful discontent. But temptation is no less powerful among the rich and famous, who may appear to lack nothing. One need only think of the Rich Man and Lazarus. His riches were a temptation. "Keep everything for you and yours. Take no heed of the annoying beggar at your front door."

A Rich Young Ruler also comes to mind. The affluent adult is told by the Master to rid himself of those possessions, and for the kingdom's sake, "Come. Follow me" (Matt 19:21; Mark 10:18). The man became crestfallen, and walked away discouraged. His ideas about service on his own terms were rejected. An often overlooked part of this story is the fact that Jesus, though he "loved him," simply let him go. The temptation to do good gave way to the overwhelming temptation to continue to define himself in terms of his material possessions.

The basic Greek word for temptation is peirasmos. It appears nineteen times in the New Testament. It is not a light or frivolous concept. Rather, it always implies suffering, trial, dread, or something ominous. It correctly belongs in the 12 insidious Problems of Evil. When Jesus taught disciples so to pray, he was declaring that the words were not for them only. Every disciple must avoid temptation even while remembering that temptation for the Lord stopped only when he breathed his last. What then for us?

Temptation is not a sin. Succumbing to it is! And yet for Christians, it is a paradoxical reality. God has created us so that maturation in faith, which he demands, can occur only by resisting and overcoming the tempting trials. Our developmental path as believers should take us to the place at which the power of temptation decreases as triumphant faith increases. Even then we cannot boast. We must remember that "Our strength comes from the Lord" (Ps 121: 2, et al.).

With that divine help we strive and struggle to reach a place at which we confidently proclaim that we cannot be tempted anymore! Even if that is an impossible attainment, we nonetheless acknowledge it as our spiritual goal.

In the age to come, temptation will be destroyed forever. In that world, we will join the assembly of "just persons made perfect" (Heb 12: 21). We will need to be tempted no more, for the agape love of God will have accomplished its saving purpose and we shall be perfect and holy before Him.

Can The Church Create Evil?

T he short, unfortunate answer to the question asked here is, "Yes. Of course." This is true because of the historic dilemma of the church: it is a "divine" institution placed in the hands of sinful humanity. What else could be expected? And if not for the restraining power and influence of the Holy Spirit, the pages of ecclesiastical history might be more sordid and disappointing than, in many places, they are. Gratefully, that history is transparent for the most part, and can be accessed by anyone interested in such things.

At the same time, the church has been, by any accounting, dispensing the love and grace of its God. History is also brimming with such examples, too numerous to cite. The Christian church has had a moral and social impact which is literally impossible to calculate. It has typically followed gospel teaching here, by not seeking or desiring accolade or recognition. Most saints and disciples have served for good and righteous reasons.

But I will not now detail the greatness of the servant church, for I am writing about the far less complimentary reality. It is transparently the case that individual Christians can create, perpetrate, and perpetuate all kinds of evil. Certainly, then, such actions can be done en masse, with the net effect of the Church giving birth to institutional evil. This becomes a perfect example of Transpersonal Evil, and takes its place among principalities, thrones, and powers which promote and spread pervasive evil (Eph 6:12).

Recalling the definition of Transpersonal Evil, in The Twelve Problems of Evil, it is unmistakably the case that these negativities may not be attributable to one or many individual persons. Rather, they take on a life of their own, now institutionalized and legalized, preserving their influence in subtle, insidious ways. This "codified" evil may reach a point among believers at which it is actually thought good or righteous. It can literally and shockingly be equated with the very will of God.

Sadly, I can present many examples which answer my question. I will confine myself to three only, but thereby convincingly make my point.

One: the Church has too often claimed for itself the power to dispense or to withold the eternal grace of God. Some Christian institutions claim to this day that their theology, liturgy, organization, and human "personnel" are integrally involved in, and essential for, determining the eternal salvation of human beings. Many groups teach that, "Outside the church there is no salvation." They mean, of course, "Outside the church as we define it."

They self-righteously employ the question, "What must I believe and do in order to be saved?" They then proceed to give the waiting world the airtight answers. In this they act as if they themselves hold the "keys of the kingdom of heaven" (Mt 16:19), and will open the doors only to the duly obedient.

I became a Christian late in my teenage years, in a fellowship that taught a rather simple "Plan of Salvation." This, of course, was for those who had reached the difficult to determine "age of accountability." It was a very preachable five finger exercise: hear, believe, repent, confess, be baptized. It was easily understood, persuasive enough, and offered Biblical texts for each step in the required process. But in actuality it was a six finger exercise, for the next step was obviously this: be faithful unto death. That command is non-controversial until any church begins telling its members everything they must believe and do in order to be faithful.

I discovered, for example that in the new community I needed to read and understand the Bible almost exactly as did elders and church leaders. There was very little room for flexibility in discussing the essential topics: the origin of faith, mode of baptism, church polity, eschatology, even the place of instrumental music in worship. Holding views contrary to establishment beliefs could label one "unsound in the faith." There were social, interpersonal consequences, as well.

My experience is not at all unique. Obviously I left that church in time, grateful that in it I had "come to Christ," and sad to leave behind many wonderful saints. I chose not to stay and "fight it out;" I redefined my own personal ministry.

When I reflect on my limited knowledge of ecclesiastical history, I can readily see that untold millions of believers have been spiritually enchained in churches which have held their eternal souls in stifling and oppressive dependence. As well-meaning as much of this may have been, the evidence of a genuine church-manufactured servility and bondage is apparent to the present hour.

This analysis can be even more distressing. Where theological beliefs are known to be purely human creations, the demand for believer acceptance and compliance can be doubly fraudulent and evil.

Two: I should comment on the monumental and devastating problem of Biblical Fundamentalism. I make two points only from what could be a lengthy book. This: fundamentalism as a view of Scripture cannot be supported by Scripture. The standards for establishing that the holy text is inspired, inerrant, and infallible must be discovered and derived from secondary, non-Biblical sources. A most honest question follows immediately: What is the origin of *those* standards; how are they determined to be inspired, inerrant, or infallible? "Canon" is a Greek word meaning "measure" or "rule." Whence the yardstick for determining that canon, the books of our Bible?

Those of us who comfortably employ historical-critical methodology in Biblical interpretation are often accused of having a low view of Scripture. I hold that, on the contrary, few reverence the text more than scholars who laboriously pore over manuscripts, parchments, ancient languages, fragments, and sources. Critical scholarship simply values and cherishes the sacred text in ways quite different from fundamentalists. Perhaps unwittingly, these good persons rely heavily on critical scholarship to produce the translations then bound in leather, which they hold so dear.

This, too. For all their high claims about the one way to correctly view the Bible, fundamentalist scholars are notoriously unable to agree on some of its basic meaning and interpretation. On very many topics in Systematic Theology, fundamentalists hold different positions. That is not arguable, but is an illuminating fact. It does raise the question: why is the fundamentalist view of sacred literature so vitally important if it does not facilitate an essential unity in interpretation? I have been a fundamentalist, inflexible and cocksure. This entire situation is not good for the church, and leads to the divisions condemned roundly in the New Testament (John 17:21; 1 Cor 1:10).

Three: there is a long and checkered history of the church's relationship to secular government. Throughout its existence it has tried to define these parameters. This is not the place to explore that fascinating topic, other than to make the point in answer to the question of this essay. I ask, "Can the church create evil in determining its relationship to worldly power and government?" The answer is a loud, "Yes!"

If the church does not maintain a safe spiritual distance from such power, it may tacitly endorse unjust governmental activity, thereby lose its identity, and shamelessly compromise itself. There is a very long history of the church not speaking "truth to power," but dancing hand in hand, abetting many pernicious evils. In so doing, the church clearly partners with, and endorses, programs and policies that are contrary to the will of God.

In our era, this plays out when any church organization or denomination proclaims that the most precise and comprehensive definition of Christian principles is to be found incorporated in the Platform of a particular political party. The individual Christian may then logically conclude that the best, most effective way to "change the world" is to work feverishly—not for the church— but for the party. Members of any other party are often deemed less faithful, even labelled non-Christian.

This reality is devastating to Christian unity, for obvious reasons. But the larger issue may be the most sinful, if it is implied and suggested that "our hope is in the elected government." This is an extremely subtle form of idolatry, with which the church has always had to deal. It can be a deeply engrained sin and evil, difficult to identify and then to eradicate. Someone rightly said that if Christians were as fervent in their passion for faith matters as they are about politics, the world would be changed in one generation!

It is exquisite irony that the church can create, perpetrate, and perpetuate evil in the world. To be sure, however, there was never a pristine, pure, innocent New Testament church. All Christians are heirs to its greatness, but heirs to its foibles and sin, as well. That sobering reminder tells believers that in no age, including ours, can we align ourselves with an organization that is completely in compliance with every dictate from Almighty God. Recognizing that gives disciples all the more impetus and desire to present to Christ a holy bride (Eph 5:27; 2 Cor 11:2). Evil and sin do not exist only in "the world!"

Animal Pain

Some years ago I was reflecting on the status of animals before the Fall. I wrote a rather bad poem with this last stanza:

> But all was "good" someone replies.
> Then ask the deer gone made from flies.
> A mangled antelope could tell
> Before the Fall there was a Hell.

I made the assumption that even before Adam took his famous bite, some animals were carnivores, living on the flesh of other creatures.

Remembering the story of Peter and the command to, "Get up, kill, and eat", (Acts 10), I wondered if God had not given the same biological, instinctual "command" to many of her created animals. Nature truly lives by "tooth and claw" as Alfred Lord Tennyson wrote in his classic poem, "In Memoriam, A. H. H."

Is animal pain and suffering, regardless of its origin, a theological problem? Yes, it is, even as it has been given pitiful little attention among religious thinkers in the West. It is, nevertheless, one of the genuine Twelve Problems of Evil, and rightfully so. Who can argue otherwise?

Some have! For all his brilliance, Rene Descartes had some very rough intellectual edges. One was his mindless notion that animals are just spiritless machines. Without a soul, he apparently reckoned, they are not able to "feel." They can, therefore, be subjected to any kind of testing or experimentation in the name of science. A common practice for several centuries was vivisection, cutting open live animals for research purposes. Someone declared that the poor animal cries were only "the grating of the animal machine," as if the creatures were made of bolts and wire and metal. What is grating is the inhumanity in such a practice and statement.

We moderns are, however, seemingly unclear about animal pain and suffering, and what to make of it. We hunt in order to preserve herds, place animals in zoos to enrich the species, and kill various game to provide meat for our tables and also for our pets. We do all this as we tearfully cringe to see footage of predatory attacks on young mammals on the Serengeti Plain of Africa. Many other such scenes create strong emotion, but the tender feelings can give way to fearsome rage when we see poaching or other acts of indiscriminate killing or maiming.

The relationship between taking animal life for food, and animal suffering and death for other reasons, is fraught with theological implications. The Christian Church has always taught that slaughtering animals for food is not an unrighteous thing. In the Old Testament there could have been no cultic practice without a daily bloody sacrifice of all kinds of living animals. Jewish religious leaders were confident that these rituals were commanded by God himself.

But there are, decidedly, other issues than religious approval for what can only be termed animal pain. These creatures are human-like in the various ways they suffer. They lose their young, contract horrific disease, and die in accident, fall, calamity. And they are still deemed invaluable and essential for all kinds of research, some of which is highly questionable and discomfiting, but doubtless saves both human and animal life.

The highest ethical standards must be brought to bear in dealing with every area of animal experimentation, death, capture, or slaughter. It is only humane to think this way, and it is completely Christian to adamantly demand it.

The "Theology of Animal Care" has yet to be formulated precisely, but it only awaits the attentive input of passionate believers. Many often competing voices are now raised in an attempt to define ethics in this important field. We do well to listen concernedly, claiming the appropriate place for our faith which affirms that "the Lord God made them all."

We cannot definitively "solve" this Problem, any more than we can the others in this larger project. But we must recognize it as legitimate and authentic. Pain, suffering, and death among these creatures must be a regular and informed part of our theology and practice of Godly living. These truly are God's creatures—not ours. They must be viewed, nurtured, and cared for accordingly.

Evil And The Sweet Illogic
Of C. S. Lewis

————

I have never been a panting devotee of C. S. Lewis. I have not been much of a detractor, either. My concerns about certain areas of his thought, especially evil, appear below. I am aware that I am critiquing one who, if Protestantism had such a classification, would surely be "Saint C. S. Lewis of Oxbridge." I mean no impertinence here, and will begin with some comments related to my genuine appreciation for who he was and what he did.

C. S. Lewis dutifully fought in the trenches on the Western Front in World War 1. He was Irish by birth, but felt that he must support the English and Allied efforts to defeat the Central Powers.

Furthermore, he was wounded in battle and carried shrapnel in his body until years later when it was surgically removed. He wrote a great deal about his experiences which, understandably troubled him for years. During the war, he was, of course, a devout atheist. The slaughter and carnage of Christian soldier against Christian soldier did not bring him closer to any god, real or imagined. Faith would come later. He saw evil "up close and personal."

Lewis became a great scholar of the literature of the Middle Ages, and wrote voluminously about it. I possess a Master of Arts in Medieval History and have much appreciated his contributions, which are read and studied to this day.

C. S. apparently displayed some behaviors that ought to endear him to anyone who prefers their saints with a slightly tarnished halo. He drank lots of alcohol, smoked, was rowdy, and had an interesting relationship with women. As a don, he was loved by some students, not so much by others. He was generous to a fault and cherished his relationship with his brother, Warren. He took exceptional care of his wife, dying from cancer. Lewis himself died much too soon, aged sixty-four, in 1963. His legacy will never die, regardless of how it is examined. His thirty books astound in many ways.

He introduced generations of readers, young and old, to the idea of transcendent worlds. He populated those realms with strange, frightening, or wonderful creatures, but left open the possibility that such worlds might be inhabited by the living God and all her saints. Lewis and his friend, J. R. R. Tolkien, were followed by countless others who created prodigious amounts of literature, video games, and movies, where audiences comfortably move between multiple dimensions. This is a highly significant phenomenon for reintroducing people to the plausibility of such realms, to the serious detriment of positions taken by die-hard empiricists. This world may not be all there is! C. S. Lewis taught us that again, and we listened.

I do have some criticisms, even if they are gentle! I knew Lewis and I would not be bosom buddies after reading *The Great Divorce*. Despite his lifelong personal and literary preoccupation with "love," he could not bring himself to affirm that God is loving enough to save everyone. He took the familiar position that human "freewill" is more powerful than God's persuasive determination to save. Therefore, the evil of defiant wills is forever coexistent with God. As a Universalist, I find this a totally unacceptable theology. God is quite capable of sustaining and honoring human freedom, even as she effects, through grace, whatever changes are necessary for humans to "come to God."

In the Screwtape books, I cannot determine whether Lewis was having so much fun that he forgot the utter seriousness of the topic entwined as it is with demonic evil. He creates interesting literary figures, then writes as if, in fact, he is "doing theology." This is unfortunate. I suppose Lewis believed in a devil possessing the same status like unto ours. But that is not the urgent theme for humans. Temptation is. It is one of the significant Problems of Evil.

The almost cutesy schemes of Screwtape and Wormwood are inexcusably inadequate in approximating the depth of dread and terror found in the Greek word for temptation, peirosmos. I do not think Jesus met Screwtape in the Temptation Narratives in the Gospels, nor on the countless other occasions where he was "tempted in all points as are we" (Heb 4:15).

Much has been made of Lewis' argument that Jesus was either a liar, or lunatic, or lord. Others have recently added another "L" word, legend, meaning he had no real "historical" existence. His story is a creative fiction. Lewis' version of this preachment is from *Mere Christianity* in 1952, though he first spoke it in 1942. Lewis' conclusion was that Jesus is/was Lord.

But surely Lewis does not intend to imply that this kind of syllogistic thinking is how anyone actually comes to faith. Coming to believe is a complicated matter, largely mysterious. Syllogisms and logical calculations always emerge in believers' minds *after* their experience of faith. And according to Lewis' own account in *Surprised By Joy*, he did not "come to Jesus" by figuring it out logically. He knew better.

If Lewis' "proof" is a syllogism, the premises cannot be proved, and therefore the conclusion is false. If anyone did, in theory, profess faith based on a syllogism, then determine its falsehood, where would faith be thereafter?

In his book, *The Problem of Pain*, Lewis writes about human suffering, animal pain, and eternal hell. His conclusions are what all believers know: the existence of these things does not keep us from faith in God. He was right to put animal pain in the mix of things evil and needing remediation. It is one of the Twelve Problems of Evil. Animals were, apparently, important to Lewis and rightly so.

At the end of this book, he came to rely on his wonderfully articulated views of transcendence. God can "see all" and we cannot. That is indeed a great part of our comforting faith. But sadly,

Lewis leaves an eternal hell "out there somewhere" for an all-seeing God to view forever. That, theologically, will not do.

We have all loved C. S. Lewis and recognize his unique influence over the decades. His breadth of thought and learning seems unbounded, and everything he wrote is worth a careful reading. Our debt to him is immeasurable.

It was the case, nevertheless, that the British "flight into faith" during the horrors of World War II, aided so powerfully by Lewis, was followed by a literal stampede away from faith when the hostilities ceased. He, of course, shares no blame for that, but since he lived until 1963, he witnessed the beginnings of that mass exodus. It continues all over Europe to this very day.

There is something quite appealing in his brand of "Mere Christianity." If it is "too mere," however, one need hardly bother with serious theology or the institutional church. I have said loudly, and do again here, that Christian Universalist Theology may yet have something to offer for reorienting all things ecclesiastical. Lewis' views to the contrary, notwithstanding!

Human Incompletion

Longevity in human life varies greatly all over the globe. Life expectancy in some countries is less than fifty years, in others approaching eighty. Some lives are deemed rich and full even if short in number of years. Others are bleak and barren even into a ninth or tenth decade.

In their autumn years, many people state things like this: "If I had it to do over again, I would . . . ." Or this: "I wish I had spent my life. . . ." Sometimes the sentences are finished in words that are less than serious, but sometimes they are pensive and filled with a legitimate and sad regret. There is, it is realized, no doing it over. Life has come and gone. One must live with the gnawing feeling of deficiency, perhaps heartfelt remorse.

I maintain that regardless of the reason, the internal or external constraint or restraint, incompletion of our limitless human potential is a Problem of Evil.

Almost every parish minister has looked out over a cemetery with wonderment. Who were these departed? What were their hopes and fears, joys and disappointments, triumphs and tragedies? One such non-clergy was the English poet, Thomas Gray. In his "Elegy Written In a Country Churchyard," published in 1751, he meditated on those lying under the sometimes illegible tombstones. Could they have been great leaders and agents of change for good? Great poets, scholars, statesmen—he wonders. He acknowledges that all classes of person, rich and poor, noble and common, end in the same small plot of land. Cemeteries are the great democracy.

The poem is dark and evocative, but contains some of the most beautiful lines in English verse. This one is memorable:

> Full many a gem of purest ray serene
> The dark unfathomed caves of ocean bear:
> Full many a flower's born to blush unseen,
> And waste its sweetness on the desert air.

One interesting fact about Gray may place him in the category of human incompletion. Though his "Elegy" was extremely popular, he actually published only thirteen poems in his entire fifty-four years of life. We wonder why.

For much of my career I was bivocational in healthcare and parish ministry. I held a license as a Nursing Home and Assisted Living Administrator for over twenty-five years. I have been associated with facilities wherein resided engineers, physicians, and United States Senators, living next door to illiterate residents of equally noble employment. They were all in the great shared conglomerative unity of issues related to human demise and end of life.

I had known the work of poet and writer Kenneth Koch, but was moved by his narrative, *I Never Told Anybody*. Using a nursing home as his laboratory, he described how residents reacted to discovering poetry so late in life. With his tutoring they created some quality verse which he subsequently published in his book. The wistful title is self-explanatory. The love, the potential, the desire was always there—but "I never told anybody!"

One of the greatest American Unitarian clergy was A. Powell Davies. Scholar, author, activist, and preacher, he did much to inform the nation and the world about the American Unitarian Association. He died in 1957, a few years before the merger of the AUA and the Universalist Church of America in 1961. His many books on liberal religion are read to this day.

One of his great sermons dealt profoundly with human incompletion. He titled it, "The Lives We Almost Live." His homilies nearly always ended with a strong, memorable admonition or blessing. This sermon ended:

> We could live those lives we nearly live. In our moments of deliberate thought we know beyond all question that no alternative is worth considering. We know that in the few short years we spend here it is folly to do anything less. The call is strong within us—the call to live. To live as we might live.[1]

Earlier in that sermon, he had written movingly: "Judas nearly decided not to betray Jesus." Almost!

There are any number of reasons why human capacity and capability are not maximized. Some are within control, others are not. Truly our species must be viewed with awe at its vast potential in every area of life.

I well understand that few persons—almost none—obtain their highest possible level of achievement. That is patently obvious. But I strongly maintain that almost every force that results in human incompletion is evil. Who would not agree with Rev. Davies: we can all envision aspects of the lives we almost live!

---

1. A. Powell Davies, *The Temptation to be Good*, Beacon Press, Boston, MA, page 75

Does God Take Human Life?

The question asked here is not intended to shock, but to invite every disciple to engage in this most serious conversation. I suspect that every believer in our Christian God has confronted the issue, and either secretly or in open discussion wondered if indeed God takes human life.

One of the most disconcerting aspects of the Problem of Evil is that it raises several questions that cause intense spiritual and psychological discomfort, even distress. I have earlier written about "ambivalence," but here I boldly go deeper.

If non-believers taunt with questions about basic and fundamental "belief in God," we true believers must deal with another list of questions and issues altogether. We practice our perplexing faith with "eyes wide open" vis-a-vis all the unwelcome facts which are ever before us, invasive and unsettling.

The point has been made that God creates and sustains evil in the world. The next logical step is to inquire into God's direct involvement in the Twelve categories. Specifically, does God, by her own initiation, cause particular manifestations of evil? Genesis declares that God speaks the worlds into being. Can it be said that God, by divine fiat, speaks into reality the visitations of evil which afflict the earth and all its creatures?

I have also said that this book is a "Bible study." Here, I will speak to only one question which has both a definite Biblical answer, but also hugely troubling implications for Christian spiritual response and accompanying devotion. The question has been posed: "Does God, by direct, intentional action, cause the death of persons?" I can now add, "some persons, or all persons?" What does Christian theology say? What does the Bible teach? Let us take a brief look.

The Old Testament is full of examples of death attributed directly to God. The writers do not blanch at the idea of reporting such details. The examples are, in fact, so numerous that I need not list them. That Jewish history extends over many centuries, and scribes and prophets portray a God who can almost routinely bless today and take life tomorrow. The nation of Israel lived in this tension, which rightly evolved into one experiential definition of "the fear of the Lord."

New Testament history is compressed to less than one hundred years. Understanding God through the Incarnation of Jesus Christ gave new insights into the "heart of God." New Testament writers had less time to reflect on the Problem of Evil and the related question of whether God destroys human life. That kind of issue would be left for latter day believers trying to determine the innumerable implications from such an unlikely fact as God appearing in the flesh.

However, the God who "kills" persons did not disappear. Luke would have us believe that the direct action of deity took the lives of Ananias and Sapphira (Acts 5), and of King Herod (Acts 12). Paul seems convinced that improper partaking of the Lord's Supper had led to supernaturally-inflicted death (1 Cor 11:30). And the bloody battles and triumphant victories of the Book of Revelation make no sense whatsoever without the active involvement of God and her knight-like Son, Jesus.

More liberal disciples might say that the Biblical attribution to God of such horrific events is entirely baseless evidentially. And even if such things occurred, the ancient peoples were merely justifying their own brutal actions by referring them to a divine involvement or command. Most conservative interpreters would loudly demur, claiming that the events transpired exactly as they were written. No further comment is needed.

It must be stated that regardless of what is believed, there could never be "conclusive evidence" of God's direct action, aside from whatever evidence is thought trustworthy from those Bible scenes and stories. Affirmations one way or the other are "faith statements," and ultimately turn on one's view of Scripture and the God therein revealed. Another approach to this most challenging question can offer helpful insight. If there are three essential views of Christian Eschatology and life in an age to come, what can be gleaned about God by looking there?

Many believe in annihilationism, or eternal destruction. The evil are judged, found wanting, and then exterminated forever. Who does this final exterminating? It is certainly God.

Many believe that evil persons are not destroyed, but are consigned to a place of everlasting torment. Who makes this final determination and disposition of these wretched souls? It is God. In this, God does not utterly destroy, as in annihilationism. Here God sustains an environment designed solely to separate and punish the wicked of the world. Some think this actually appears frightfully worse than any form of death.

There are those who believe in Universalism, the final restoration of all persons in a heavenly beatitude. In this view, of course, there is no Endtime issue relating to God and death. All are saved to live forevermore. Death itself is destroyed. Eternal life is the strong emphasis.

It seems correct to wonder if those believing in either eternal destruction or eternal hell are not more favorably inclined to accept the idea of the God who openly takes human life. Their Endtime views make some earthly events of death and destruction pale in companion to what occurs in their visions of eternity.

One other response to our question demands attention here. This very disturbing matter may incline Christians toward embracing the historic faith of Deism—at least partially and temporarily. That theology has several tenets, but the one related here is its teaching that God is not "personally" involved in the affairs of the world. To be sure, God creates the cosmos, and observes all that transpires, but does not intervene or interfere. Deism may appear to spare God from the direct act of taking life, but it does not. God (who else?) is ultimately responsible for empowering any intermediary so assigned to accomplish this deadly task. Simply put, the God of Deism is not the God of the Bible, and cannot be considered in discussing this issue. Improperly understood, Deism has its appeal, but a flight in its direction helps only emotionally and psychologically, not theologically or spiritually.

Christian faith has confidently affirmed that all life is a divine gift, and is held firmly in the palm of God's hand. But serious thinkers acknowledge the limiting and confining outlines in any human-led discussion of God and death. Earthlings cannot claim to know or to declare what they do not. To do so is spiritual dishonesty.

Believers must quickly and humbly remember that we are dealing here with the Triune God Almighty. One of the greatest Biblical understatements is surely this: "His ways are not our ways; her thoughts are not our thoughts" (Is 55:8). Many other verses loudly proclaim the infinite distance between divine action and human understanding.

Does God cause human death? After thousands of years of believers looking heavenward, searching for answers, in 1563, the Heidelberg Catechism offered a beautiful and calming statement of hope. It maintained that the entire content of faith should begin with the Christian's fundamental and foundational awareness. And so the authors wrote this:

Question 1: "What is our only comfort in life and death? That I, with body and soul, both in life and in death, am not my own, but I belong unto my faithful Savior Jesus Christ."

To say that God "called home" a ninety-year old saint, after a long life well lived, is one thing. To say that God "called home" a three-year old child after a long struggle with cancer, is quite another. We are, in the end, simply left in that existential uncertainty and tension. It is, after all, our human condition and lot.

Does God cause human death? Christians must be appropriately wary when answering that and similar questions.

Our God Who Suffers

The last item in the list of the Twelve Problems of Evil is my declaration that the immanent Triune God is immersed in the historical outworking of every aspect of this world, and as a result she suffers. It could not be otherwise given God's eternal desire to be in fellowship with all of her creatures. This implies a profound familiarity with each of us as we live our lives on this earth. If God will do everything necessary to redeem each one in the age to come, it seems perfectly clear that God has an intense Mother-Father caring concern for all his children in this and every age. If that is true, God knows the joy, pain, suffering, and sorrow of these beloved, and participates in every aspect, even if in very mysterious ways. Surely, God must continually suffer as lives play out in this wonderful world, which is so interspersed with overwhelming evil.

As always, the Only-begotten Son helps us here. The suffering God is made visible in the Christian doctrine of the Incarnation, wherein the Trinity freely chooses to take on flesh and "walk among us." The beautiful Statement of Faith of the United Church of Christ declares it well: "God seeks in holy love to save all people from aimlessness and sin." Love's mission is salvific, but humans constantly reject the overtures of love, including that of the dramatic earthly appearance of a Redeemer. When creatures spurn, resist, and repudiate agape love, the reality of God's suffering can only be more poignant.

Scores of New Testament verses are illustrative of God's watchful, compassionate concern for all. Presented is a God who sees, takes notice, and cares deeply. No one disputes these divine characteristics, but is it demonstrable that God actually suffers? It is easy to make theological statements, as I have done. Am I simply conferring on the divine God attributes, traits, and emotions that are purely and solely human?

That would be called "anthropomorphizing." We do it all the time, especially when around our pets and other animals. We utilize language as if our words were the medium of understanding for them. Animal behaviors indicate that we are "communicating," and that is an amazing thing, which certainly endears them to us even more.

As we use our only resource, anthropomorphizing, can we draw any legitimate conclusions about God and suffering? It was, not surprisingly, a topic of great theological interest in the early centuries of the church. Some curious "fathers," using some "big" theological terms, exhaustively debated the matter. After a few hundred years, the issue was sensibly settled: God has "passion" and God can suffer in Godself.

The alternative view—that God cannot "feel"—would have been disastrous for Christian theology, and a complete abandonment of much basic and fundamental Biblical teaching. It was an era when theology was almost wholly subsumed under Greek philosophical categories. We must thank the Holy Spirit for strong guidance in leading the church and its Councils into right thinking, what we call "Orthodoxy."

The central focus of that corrective thinking was, of course, the Scriptures. What kind of God was portrayed there? If it was deemed problematic for God to possess passion, what about the whole concept of love, the highest divine passion?

Though God's revelation in Holy Writ is sketchy and incomplete, we can offer some strong convictions about this issue. I share them with a minimum of supporting data, but they are all more than plausible.

One: it "cost" God a great deal to create the world in the first place. Creation was clear evidence of a deity willing to eternally self-limit, withholding vast divine powers in order to produce and sustain what has appeared, including the human species.

Two: At some point in the world's unfolding, God chose to reveal himself in an effort to communicate love and commandment, law and gospel. God's goal was to "raise up" children into a people who would then bless all nations of the earth. The image is apt, for Israel had a very hard time going from its childhood to adulthood. Father-Mother God came regularly to chide, correct, punish, but always to bless. If God showed her "emotional life" through the prophets, she wept more than once over her unfaithful but chosen people.

Three: the Jewish nation never fulfilled the mandate to "bless all peoples of the earth," until that idea was compressed and actualized in the coming person and work of Jesus. If, as with prophets, Jesus reflects the true "heart of God," then the Holy One reacts to the sin of peoples with anger but also tearful complaint and parental compassion.

Four: Jesus on the cross cries, "My God, my God." It is impossible to imagine or suggest that God's perceived absence was genuine indifference or callous disregard. In actuality, God was never closer to the Son. Surely, there is unfathomable suffering here.

Five: I believe God suffers in our time in many, many ways. Here are a few. Humans sin boldly and horrifically. We refuse to mature in faith. God's blessings are not recognized or acknowledged. Her blessings are rejected outright. Christianity is presented to the world in a shoddy, even tawdry way. Humans devastate the planet and its creatures. God's restraining of vast evil among nations is dismissed as infantile thinking. The faith is made into a purely political ideology. God is intentionally not worshipped.

I could go on and on. It is not enough to say that these, and a myriad other examples, merely displease God. The term needed is "suffer."

Six: Christians instinctively proclaim that God has "feelings," but rarely do they comment on anything like suffering. Roadway billboards and placards in the stands at major sporting events announce, "God Loves You," and "John 3: 16." In my American South, I have many times seen those words painted on the rooftops or the sides of very old barns. For those entirely convinced of God's eternal agape, that is a not so subtle evangelism!

Occasionally, the message of these proclaimers is, "Christ died for your sins." That is more affecting, to be sure, intended to convey the cost of death by crucifixion.

Seven: My next point is that Almighty God has revealed enough, in and through our imperfect human languages, for us to trust the characterizations about God's anger, love, and pain. They may well be anthropomorphic descriptions, but they are ours to study, ponder, and cherish. Some things attributed to God must be reviewed through the fact of the Incarnation. Not every recorded event is "of God" or worthy of God.

But we have no "heavenly language," and have no access to one. John Calvin was no doubt correct to state that in the Bible, God is speaking to us in "baby talk." That is quaint and cute, but absolutely not wrong. Unless God willingly comes down to share her life with ours, we should know nothing of a divine reality. Joyfully, God is always "coming to us."

And this in closing: The Problems of Evil were never a "problem" for God. Though she did not reveal to humans any information that would clarify the mystery, she was totally and completely in ultimate control of every aspect of the unfolding drama of world history. She is now orchestrating the divine outcome, as a conductor leads instrumentalists through a grand symphony. He is not predestinating the players, but has the skill to produce a beautiful, breath-taking performance at the end.

This is the undeniable corollary. Christian theology must affirm that the Triune God in pure, free, sovereign grace, mediated through agape love, willingly chooses to be vulnerable to the plight of her human creatures, and in that vulnerability suffers in ways unknowable to those creatures.

Our holy God determined to spend the entire history of the cosmos in this declension of power in order to obtain and express an eternal exaltation of love. That love will be showered on every beloved child forever. When we are all in that beatitude, God's suffering will cease!

We Are "Children"

In 1986, a play by Mark Medoff was adapted for the big screen and made into a movie. It was a "hit," garnering many nominations and awards, including Best Actress from both the Academy of Motion Pictures and the Golden Globes. I did not see the play, but thought the movie excellent, worthy of all its accolades and plaudits.

The movie starred William Hurt, Marlee Matlin, and a stellar supporting cast. It was set off the coast of Maine, where Hurt went to teach at a School for the Deaf. Matlin was a hearing impaired custodian, with whom Hurt became infatuated. The interesting story unfolds from there.

The play and the movie were perfectly titled, "Children of a Lesser God." It was not in the least theological in content, but the provocative title suggested a profound concept for those of us dealing with the Problems of Evil. The implication from that title is transparent: deaf persons are the creation of a lesser God, one who could not endow hearing, or who herself was hearing impaired.

In my family a loving couple have four beautiful "natural" children. They have also adopted four more. One has no arms; one is deaf and blind; one has no feet and webbed hands. Those children are flourishing in an environment determined to see them grow up and succeed in life. I marvel and bow down before such service, done, in this case, in the name of holy Christ.

Are these delightful, wonderful, real life creatures children of a lesser God, one who could not quite produce "perfect" offspring from the mother's womb?

If we concluded that, because of the Problems of Evil, we were all children of such a God, we would be woefully mistaken. Mistaken, that is, in view of the teachings of the entire Judeo-Christian tradition of faith and practice. That theology presents a God who is not "less than," but is rather the loving and caring God above all "other Gods before me" (Ex 20:3). Believers affirm the truth of that, even as we wrestle with the hurtful realities of pervasive, overwhelming evil. We struggle on with the meaning of life and death. In doing so, we often forget the blessings, beauty, and richness surrounding us. We are sinners, after all.

If we deny, downplay, or trivialize the reality of evil, we are naive, callous, and feckless. If we obsess about it, we are paralyzed and ineffective. One of the unspoken goals and benefits of the Christian faith is its offer and gift of "spiritual balance." That blessing is as old as the Old Testament: "though I walk through the valley of the shadow of death . . . ,"—and we all will. It is as new as the precious words of Christ, "I am with you always."

The wondrous irony is that the God who creates and sustains evil, lovingly goes with us through it all, and even helps us triumph over it. No mystery is deeper or more unfathomable! No love is greater!

We are not children of a lesser God, but we are children. Called that repeatedly in the Scriptures of our faith. It is the correct term. Children assuredly refers to how depthlessly we are loved and treasured by our heavenly Parent. Children also refers to how vast is the mind of God, and how limited is our human ability to understand his mysterious ways.

That is, then, our plight, not to be changed on this earth, but to be eternally changed when we burst into the glory of the living Holy One.

Children of a lesser God? No. We are children of the Most High Triune God!

And one day this very God said: "I have seen the afflictions of my people, and I have come down to help" (Ex 3: 7–8). These two verses contain the essence of the Problem of Evil: the suffering of the earth, the caring concern of the heavenly Parent, and the promise that one day—if not today—one day, our loving Father-Mother God will come as Savior. Until then we wait, we work, we watch, we worship.

Bibliography

Davies, A. Powell. *The Temptation To Be Good.* Beacon Press, 1952.

Drina, Katerina. "...One Must Imagine Sisyphus Happy." *Hektoen International Journal,* 2018.

Overbye, Dennis. "Did God Have a Choice?" *The New York Times,* 1999.

Pereto, Juli, et al. "Charles Darwin and the Origin of Life." In *Origins of Life and the Evolution of the Biosphere.* Netherlands: Springer, 2009.

www.ingramcontent.com/pod-product-compliance
Lightning Source LLC
Chambersburg PA
CBHW070504090426

42735CB00012B/2674